The Perk Paperboy

*To John —
I hope you
enjoy these little
stories —
In friendship,
Len Blackwell*

Len Blackwell

WestBow
PRESS
A DIVISION OF THOMAS NELSON

Copyright © 2010 Len Blackwell

All rights reserved. No part of this book may be used or reproduced by any means, graphic, electronic, or mechanical, including photocopying, recording, taping or by any information storage retrieval system without the written permission of the publisher except in the case of brief quotations embodied in critical articles and reviews.

WestBow Press books may be ordered through booksellers or by contacting:

WestBow Press
A Division of Thomas Nelson
1663 Liberty Drive
Bloomington, IN 47403
www.westbowpress.com
1-(866) 928-1240

Because of the dynamic nature of the Internet, any Web addresses or links contained in this book may have changed since publication and may no longer be valid. The views expressed in this work are solely those of the author and do not necessarily reflect the views of the publisher, and the publisher hereby disclaims any responsibility for them.

ISBN: 978-1-4497-0565-7 (sc)
ISBN: 978-1-4497-0567-1 (dj)
ISBN: 978-1-4497-0566-4 (e)

Library of Congress Control Number: 2010937272

Printed in the United States of America

WestBow Press rev. date: 11/19/2010

"I did not have time to read this, but once I started, I could not stop. I read until 11 p.m. and then woke up at 2:30 a.m. and finished at dawn, January 6, 2010.

This account of life in a southern hamlet, just before the horrific experience of Vietnam ended America's last era of innocence, would be of interest to any student of sociology. But in the case of this reader, its magnetism springs from the fact that I knew nearly everyone in the *Perk Paperboy* a decade later, having arrived in Perk as a history teacher in 1967. I was fascinated by the sketches of the younger Dean C.G. Odom, Sydney Alexander, Gregory Davis, Sadie Lee, and so many others. C.G. hired me. Miss Alexander's office was on the same hall as mine in the Dees Building, and Mrs. Davis showed me the squared timbers in her home that were hand hewed circa 1859 by John Perkins who gave his name to "Perkins Town." I saw Sadie Lee stick a screwdriver in an electrical socket and melt in a flash of sparkling blue fire that did no harm because it had a rubber handle. To me, reading this was like watching the first half of a movie I had already seen the ending of.

I enjoyed it thoroughly."

—Charles Sullivan, author of *Mississippi Gulf Coast Community College: A History*

"Len Blackwell has written a warm and loving account of growing up in Perkinston, Mississippi. Readers will perceive images of Tom Sawyer and Huck Finn in the author's adventures. It is a book for every family's bookshelf to be read again and again."

—George Thatcher, author of *Beach Walks*

"Barrister, scholar, statesman, raconteur, and not least, a paper boy to all manner of folks during hard times, Len Blackwell has put to paper the most wonderful memories and adventures afforded a fun-loving, precociously astute, sometimes hard-working boy lucky enough to have grown up in the friendly fold of family, neighbors, teachers and a few loveable eccentrics, reprobates and scoundrels thrown in to flavor with love, honesty and insight, the small piney woods community of Perkinston in south Mississippi."

—Thomas E. Simmons whose latest book is *Forgotten Heroes of World War II*

For readings, signings and speaking engagements, contact the author at lblackwell@cableone.net

To Leo and Silas
and grand children everywhere

Foreword

This book is not about Katrina, not about any great storm or other natural catastrophe. It is not about brutal treatment of men by other men. It is not about corruption and dishonesty. It is not about pride, arrogance, and prejudice. It is not about the rich and the famous. This book is about a young boy, his family, their neighbors and their friends; their values, the respect and affection they had for each other; their love of music, of humor and laughter and the keenness of their wit. It is about the life of "the people" in these United States and in the State of Mississippi, their simplicity, warmth and beauty, their respect for learning, as they are, a small part of what America is. There are many thousands of "Perks", (Perkinstons), towns like Wiggins, counties like Stone, filled with good people. The paper boy will introduce you to "Americans". They are good people. You will be glad to find, probably, that they are much like you.

Joel Blass
Pass Christian, Mississippi 2010

Joel Blass, a graduate of Louisiana State University School of Law, served in the United States Army in World War II and during the Korean Conflict; he returned to Wiggins, Mississippi, where he practiced law, served in the Mississippi Legislature and raised his family. He served as Professor of Law at the University of Mississippi School of Law, practiced law in Gulfport and served as a Justice on the Mississippi Supreme Court.

Contents

Foreword ix
Introduction. xiii
Author's Preface xvii
Memories. 1
Perk Paperboy. 4
Things To Do 7
A New Sound. 10
Music, Music, Music!. 13
A Little Night Music 15
Where have all the flowers gone? 18
Likely Heroes. 21
P.O.E.M. 24
Summertime 26
Swimming and Other Pastimes 29
Sunday Dinner. 31
Wood Choppers. 33
Porch Philosophy. 36
Shopping on Pine Street. 39
Ladies. 43
Pa and Dee. 46
Friends. 49
More on Mr. Lyman. 52
Stars over Ramsay Springs 55
Cars 57
Holiday Song. 59
Christmas. 61
Dees Store 63
Dogs 65
Fashion Statement 87
Gentleman and Scholar 90

Losing Your Marbles	92
Boy Scout	94
Buddies	96
Temperamental Mower	98
Problem Number One	100
Lawn Mower Lesson	102
Going on Vacation	105
Vacation Memories II	108
Little Fellows, Eccentrics and Acceptance	110
The Grill	114
Courthouse Days	116
Saving the Library	120
Tolerance	122
Annual Ball	125
Icons	128
A Night at the Opera	130
Life Is But A Dream	134
Small Miracles	137
Friends and Neighbors	140
Foxhunting Memories	142
Perk Baptist Church	146
At the Movies	149
A Lodge of Masons	152
Perk beat Pearl River!	155
I'm Still Pedaling	158
Afterword	160
Final Poem	161
A Conversation with Len Blackwell	163

Introduction

"You can't go back home to your family, back home to your childhood... back home to a young man's dreams of glory and of fame ... back home to places in the country, back home to the old forms and systems of things which once seemed everlasting but which are changing all the time, back home to the escapes of Time and Memory."

Thomas Wolfe

    The 1950s Perkinston, Mississippi, of my youth was a rural, American, idyllic landscape. Perk was a loose weave of a small agricultural school system and a junior college campus supported by a few commercial outcroppings, a Baptist church, a post office, and the Masonic Lodge. The village center was Dees General Store, a rambling wooden structure that stocked everything from sliced meats and dry goods to hardware and fishing supplies. Along the long, open porch across the front of the establishment was a bench where townsfolk and students passed the sub-tropical days, exchanging niceties, family recipes and neighborly banter, reminiscent of Mayberry RFD. Dees Store and Hershel's Gulf were the only two commercial enterprises that served the handful of folks who made up the faculty, staff and student body of the college campus. Outside of those employed or attending the college, there were perhaps a hundred local souls who logged, farmed or just lived off the sandy loam soil between Red and Ten Mile Creeks.

    We worked for the college and lived in the faculty housing on campus across the street from the old gym and just down the hill from the elementary school and the church. We were remote but very much a part of the American life. Bonanza had just launched in color, the Yankees were playing well, and we were trying our best to beat the Russians to the moon. The local buzz was much more about fishing, coon hunting, science fairs, cheerleading summer camp, and who said what on the party line.

At the time Len was tossing papers, Sandy Koufax was throwing record-breaking fast balls and Castro was overthrowing the Cuban government. The Daily Herald was our lifeline to the outer world where Hank Aaron was breaking down the color barrier in baseball, Elvis was shaking up the music world, and the Berlin Wall was being built. News from the conflict in Korea was personal and baffling, as we thought we had just fought the war to end all wars. There was no way we could have imagined the continuation of war that plagues us to this day.

And now I am going to tell you a secret. It's not about where we buried our beloved family dog, Happy, or where I removed a brick under the house and put a collection of my favorite things for safe keeping, my own personal time capsule, if you will. It's not about the first girl I kissed or about how I was "going with" a girl from Wiggins (via the telephone) and broke up with her before we ever met. No, this is something more about this thing we call home. A fact that has occurred to me of late is that when we packed up our meager belongings in the summer of 1965 and moved from Perkinston to the red-clay hills of Booneville, I would never feel the sense of being settled again. As we drove north away from the coastal plain into the strange and seemingly distant realm of our new home, I lost my sense of place, as one loses their sense of direction. I have lived here and there and have been happy in periods in certain places, but when we moved that first time, it was my last sense of being home, of knowing where home was, of being "from" somewhere. From then on, I have been living in places and never again been "from" any place.

So, as I look long into the face of my personal history, I realize what Thomas Wolfe was writing about; what the true meaning of being displaced from home feels like. And while one may never go home again, I believe through the art of stories, we can at least reflect, remember, and reminisce about a time and place held sacred in our memory, our history, and our collective shared lives.

Len has set here on paper part of our tale, some of the stories of this small and cohesive community of Perk. He watched and remembered how we lived, who we were and what our time was like. He had a unique perch from atop his bike, loaded with the news of the day, the box scores, the obituaries of family and friends, the photos of Mardi Gras, the coast fishing report and the gossip of south Mississippi, the nation and the world. Len not only delivered the news; he watched and observed the present time of a sleepy village waking up every morning, stretching and starting the day.

His stories are our stories, and what he reports is our history, the forming of our culture and a peek at a time past. This was a time when cars had big fins and TVs had antennas, when a Coke was a dime and the recycled bottle was worth a penny. It was the best of times, when we thought all the wars were over and the world was our oyster. The new party line is the internet and the old gym is being torn down, but Len's stories are forever and serve to remind us of our sense of place in this sometimes calamitous and chaotic world. If in fact we can't go home again, then we can at least journey back through this collection and reconnect with memory and emotion and our senses from scenes of that time, that place, that postage stamp of earth called Perk.

Malcolm White
Jackson, Mississippi 2010

From rural Stone County, Mississippi, Malcolm White worked his way through the ranks of the hospitality industry, which led him and his brother Hal to open one of Jackson's most celebrated gathering places – Hal & Mal's. He has been involved in many charitable endeavors. As Executive Director of the Mississippi Arts Commission, Malcolm works for the arts across the entire state, and he was instrumental to the cultural rebuilding of the Gulf Coast communities that were devastated by Hurricane Katrina

Author's Preface

This little book of stories is for newspaper carriers and people who read the newspapers they deliver. It is also for people who grew up in small towns and in the country, and who live in small communities, even in big towns and cities. The stories were originally written for my grandchildren, and some of them were published in the <u>Stone County Enterprise</u>, the weekly newspaper in Wiggins, Mississippi. If they seem a little disjointed and repetitious, that is probably the reason.

I know that much has been said lately about the death of the great tradition of newspapers in America. In a November, 2009 article in <u>Harper's</u> magazine, Richard Rodriguez said, "When a newspaper dies in America, it is not simply that a commercial enterprise has failed; a sense of place has failed." And yet we all know places where people still wait eagerly for their newspapers to be delivered, ready to have a cup of coffee and read today's story of their own community. The <u>Sun Herald</u>, successor of the newspaper that I delivered when I was a teenager, is still a robust community institution in South Mississippi that has been in continuous existence since 1884. It is hardy and hale.

Newspaper carriers are also a hardy lot in every corner of America. In his wonderful book <u>South of Broad</u>, Pat Conroy describes a carrier in Charleston, South Carolina:

> "I could lob a newspaper with either hand. When I turned left on Tradd Street, I looked like an ambitious acrobat hurling papers to my right and left as I made my way toward the Cooper River and the rising sun that began to finger the

morning tides of the harbor, to dance along the spillways of palmetto fronds and water oaks until the street itself burst into the first flame of morning."

You see, the newspaper carrier knows his terrain and her community on a very close and personal basis.

In his article in <u>Harper's</u> magazine, Richard Rodriguez says,

"Late in grammar school and into high school, I delivered the <u>Sacramento Bee</u>, a newspaper that was, in those years, published in the afternoon, Monday through Saturday, and in the morning on Sundays...

The papers were barely dry when I got them, warm to the touch and clean – if you were caught short, you could deliver a baby on newspaper. The smell of newspapers was a slick petroleum smell of ink. I would fold each paper in triptych, then snap on a rubber band. On Thursdays, the Bee plumped with a cooking section and with supermarket ads. On Sundays there was added the weight of comics, of real estate and automobile sections, and supplements like <u>Parade</u> and the television guide.

I stuffed half my load of newspapers into the canvas bag I tied onto my bicycle's handlebars; the rest went into saddlebags on the back. I never learned to throw a baseball with confidence, but I knew how to aim a newspaper well enough.
I could make my mark from the sidewalk – one hand on the handlebar – with dead-eye nonchalance.

The paper flew over my shoulder; it twirled over hedges and open sprinklers to land with a fine plop only inches from the door."

I hope there will always be newspapers and newspaper carriers, because we need the sense of community they bring to the places that they serve. They are part of the connection that neighbors still have in this country.

I love the old song by A. P. Carter, "Newsboy Jimmy Brown"; it tells about a newspaper carrier who believes he is going to Heaven:

> " I sell the morning paper sir, my name is Jimmy Brown.
> ...my mother always tells me, sir,
> there's nothing in this world to lose;
> I'll get a place in Heaven, sir, to sell the gospel news".

Now, I wouldn't say that every newspaper carrier is going to Heaven, but every one of them that I know has had an interesting journey through his or her hometown, along the way. One of my great privileges in life was to participate in the journey!

This little book is also about life in the 1950s which was a magical time for me, a kid growing up in the village of Perkinston, Mississippi. We respected institutions because we respected the men and women who comprised them. We were optimistic. Buddy Holly was still alive. In Don McLean's elegiac song "American Pie," he describes himself as a paperboy who had to deliver the news in February, 1959, that Buddy Holly had died tragically in an airplane crash, an event filled with symbolism. Indeed America changed during the next ten years following the death of Buddy Holly, whose pure and simple music typified the new rock music of the 1950s and in some ways could have been a metaphor for our relatively innocent country. I was also a paperboy who delivered papers recounting the news of that tragic event without anticipating what was to follow. I am very grateful that I had the opportunity to live where I lived when I lived during the times remembered in these stories.

I owe an enormous debt of gratitude to many friends who have helped to push this little book over the finish line. To my brother David, for telling me to detour by our hometown that wonderful autumn day and for his words of encouragement as the stories began to take form; to Kathryn Lewis and Daisha Walker and Dick O'Neal and Nell Murray and all my friends in the Telling Trees, a group started by Kathryn that actually collects and tells stories in and around Perkinston and Stone County, Mississippi, in order to keep cherished memories alive; to the Mississippi Humanties Council for providing a grant to further adaptation of the "Perk Paperboy Stories" for performance of them by the Telling Trees; to Joel Blass, a lifelong friend and hero, who contributed to my decision to become a lawyer, and for his writing the gracious and eloquent foreword to the stories; to Malcolm White, a great friend who grew up in Perkinston, shares good memories of his life there and who currently serves the people of Mississippi as Director of The Mississippi Arts Commission, for writing such a thoughtful and poignant introduction, one that captures the spirit of our hometown; to Charles Sullivan, the hardest working man in the history of history, Professor Emeritus of History at the Perkinston Campus of Mississippi Gulf Coast Community College, who serves as the official archivist of the college, who found time to read and proofread the manuscript and offered valuable suggestions to make it better and who graciously granted use of photos and captions from his own book; to my old friend Tom Simmons, a fine writer who performed the same valuable editing function; a special thank you to Stan Tiner, Editor of the <u>Sun Herald</u> the descendant of <u>The Daily Herald</u> for his kind and provocative Afterword. My dear wife, Mary, also gave the stories a final read. Thanks for your honesty. And to my law office staff for putting up with me while I was fiddling around with text, you are the best; to Thomas Nelson, Inc., and my daughter Daisy, who is one of its vice presidents, and my daughter Caroline who encouraged me and who worked in publishing and helped lure Daisy in that direction; and finally to my wife Mary, the love of my life and someone who has put up with me, given me her support, and who has been my muse for, oh, about half a century.

Gulfport, Mississippi
2010

Memories

I can't believe it– 2007– fifty (50) years since 1957, which was one of the greatest years in American history, or at least in Perkinston history. The 1950s were interesting times – it was then that I came of age (or at least <u>teen</u> age) in Perkinston, Mississippi, my home town.

I was about to enter my junior year at Perkinston Agricultural High School where we had great teachers like Miss Sydney Alexander (why I majored in English), Coach Mel Carpenter (civics in those days was a must), and principal J. V. Wentzell (a great chemistry teacher and strict administrator.)

Henry ("Goat") Rath had just perfected his football (and leadership) skills, and morale at PAHS was sky high! Coach J.V. Shiel perennially fielded winning teams, the '57 Chevrolet was the dream car of everyone (we didn't dare dream of Thunderbirds or Corvettes), and Dwight David Eisenhower was President.

The word terrorism was probably not even in the dictionary, and we prayed and said the Pledge of Allegiance in "chapel," which was a mandatory assembly we attended with the college (Perkinston Junior College) students in the auditorium. We didn't have to lock our doors.

In 1957 I was the paperboy in Perkinston, delivering <u>The Daily Herald</u> on my Western Flyer bicycle Monday through Saturday for twenty five cents a week per customer. I always made my last stop the college cafeteria where Thelma Andrews, the chef, would have a cold glass of milk and a warm cinnamon roll waiting for me. Now there is a dormitory named after Thelma, a "colored" gentleman who was a friend and who always set a good example for me.

It is trite to say it takes a village to raise a child– but think of the role models I had the opportunity to know: Casa Hatten, the assistant postmaster (business must have been brisk); J. W. Mitchell, our Perkinston Elementary School principal and scoutmaster, who took Perkinston Troop 110 to the Boy Scout National Jamboree in Valley Forge, Pennsylvania that year; Professor Eugene Clement, the great choir director, and Professor Sam Jones, one of the best band directors of all times; Jim Byrd (our assistant scoutmaster who was a World War I vet. and a great hunter– (in the woods he took <u>one</u> shotgun shell, his old single barrel Winchester, some sardines and onions for lunch, and more often than not he killed a buck); Pal Bond, who had the only service station (Gulf Oil) in town, and his successor, Herschel Breland (who delivered the mortal coup de grace to the first buck I ever shot, but gave me credit for it); Monk Jordan, who was just a great person and raised a wonderful family; Dave Sanders, a gentleman of color whose daughters babysat me and my brother; and I haven't begun to mention all the wonderful ladies like Ruby Dedeaux, Gregory Davis, Zettie Dedeaux, Myrtis Krohn, my Mom, and so many, many others.

I was a campus kid and then a courthouse kid (when my Dad served as Dean of Men at Perk and as the elected County Superintendent of Education respectively). Col. Bob Rivers, a dapper southern gentleman, was the college registrar who also taught social studies. The K.P. (Fausts Professor K.P. Faust was the renowned chemistry teacher, with Mrs. Faust his chief assistant), Susie Cooley, the French and Spanish teacher, who also taught speech, and J.J. Hayden (who later became president of the college) were all great, and at the courthouse I saw three giants: Bob Newton, Boyce Holleman and Joel Blass– all great lawyers and inspirations to a country boy.

Not long ago my brother David was visiting from Dothan, Alabama, and he wanted to ride through Wiggins and Perkinston. We revelled in the good memories, and then he suggested that we stop for a visit at the Perkinston Cemetery. Dearly beloved, it was like visiting cherished friends and loved ones as we ambled around that peaceful graveyard. There was the Dees family–Uncle Cal and his sons John and Gene and Billy Jack. There was my first grade teacher, Mrs. Jim Davis (whose Christian name was Gregory), and so many other dear essential friends and neighbors who gave me to know right from wrong and who were and are the salt of the earth. Such wisdom and kindness in them!

And the best secret they all whispered to us on our nonchalant, respectful pilgrimage: "the best days lie ahead, in the future!"

I hope you enjoy these Paperboy Stories. I know I have enjoyed remembering the great people who lived in our little village. Many lessons I learned while growing up in Perkinston have stayed with me throughout my life, and I am grateful to have been, at least for a few years, the Perk Paperboy.

All mistakes and lapses in memory are entirely mine.

Perk Paperboy

One of these days I should write a book called <u>Everything I Learned on My Newspaper Route in Perkinston</u>, because I have to say it was a real education. In the 1950s there were only two possible jobs available for a kid like me—sacking groceries at Gene Dees' store (the sign said "Dees Co. General Mdse," not "General Store" like it was in the western movies and comic books)—and that job was already taken by Dilly Easterling who performed it by day and occasionally tended bar at the Toot n' Tell It by night. The other job was to be the paperboy and deliver <u>The Daily Herald</u> newspaper.

The paperboy job was a sort of inherited position—Karl Hatten did it; then his brother Clyde; and then Bobby Burnham; then, finally, me. It was the mid-1950s, and I was a magic thirteen years old. My first fun job! Up until then, I had eked out a little spending money mowing lawns with a temperamental Sears Roebuck push mower that sometimes simply refused to crank. One time I was commissioned to mow the Perk Cemetery in the hottest part of August, and it was like navigating a rock garden, pushing a flailing machine in a gigantic sauna. Believe me, riding around on my Western Flyer was a breeze by comparison.

To say Perkinston was a quiet community in the summertime is a serious understatement. We were easily amused. Until I got on the paper route, the most excitement I can remember is the time during a rabies epidemic when a mad fox walked smack into downtown Perk, right by the old railroad depot, and my Dad took his rifle and shot him. Everybody had to stay inside, which was fine by me, as hot as it was.

The <u>Daily Herald</u> in those days was an afternoon paper, and one of the most exciting events to me was the anticipation of having <u>The Mysterious Blonde Haired Lady</u> roar up in her 1955 White Chevrolet station wagon and hurl my two twine-wrapped bundles of papers up onto the porch of the old Perk Post Office. In those days, Marilyn Monroe was regarded as an icon (at least by me) and when <u>The Blonde Haired Lady</u>, fairly glistening in her unairconditioned equipage, socked those bundles on that porch, well.... Usually about thirty minutes before The Blonde Haired Lady's estimated time of arrival, both Abner Flurry, the postmaster, and Casa Hatten, the assistant postmaster, found it vitally necessary to take a nonchalant afternoon break and come sit on the porch. Sometimes, Albert Earl McDonald, a confirmed bachelor if ever there was one, also found that time of day to be convenient for him to drop in to check his mail. Even elderly John Clayton, with his broad brimmed hat and suspenders and Uncle Jim Byrd, the WWI Vet, tall and trim in his khakis and with a twinkle in his eye, would pop by for some light conversation. The Mysterious Blonde Haired Lady, dressed in black pedal pushers and a short sleeved white blouse, would rarely say anything as she athletically hefted my paper bundles, but she would usually have a kind of wry, Mona Lisa smile generally directed toward her appreciative audience. I thought she was sensational. After she roared away, made her dusty exit, and the cloud of dust from the Chevy Wagon subsided and I took delivery of my paper bundles, for some reason everyone quickly dispersed and it was always back to business as usual.

I don't know what my fellow porch codgers did after the Blonde Haired Lady roared away because that was when my paper route began, and I was on a mission. I loaded the bundles in the canvas <u>Daily Herald</u> bag that fit over the handlebars, after freeing them from their twine bondage, and set about to deliver the news. My first stop was right down the street at Pal Bond's Gulf Service Station. Gasoline was probably about 24 9/10 cents a gallon, with full service. When I say full service, I mean the kind mentioned in the old Chuck Berry song "Too Much Monkey Business" where he says, "Working in the filling station, too many tasks; check the water, check the tires, check the oil, a dollar gas." <u>And</u>, they would sweep out the inside of your jalopy, <u>and</u> they were nice and affable and made you feel welcome! I always thought Pal was a marketing genius because there, perched on a shelf in the northwest corner inside the station was a real miracle–a television set! A great many people did not have television sets, and when the snowy black and white picture came on, it was hard not to stop there and buy your gas.

I would leave several papers at Pal's station, some of them for people I didn't know–shipyard workers and other people who just preferred to pick up their papers there on the way home. They always left the money for me in an envelope, and I never missed a penny, they were so utterly and reliably creditworthy. Believe it when I tell you that a paperboy quickly learns who pays on time and who doesn't.

After leaving Pal's, my route meandered down toward Red Creek, under the famous Perkinston overhead bridges. I learned from Professor Charles Sullivan's great history of the College that Perkinston is the <u>only</u> place between the Coast and Jackson where U.S. Highway 49 crosses the tracks of what was then the Illinois Central Railroad.

Those bridges lofted travelers on Highway 49 over our little village, and while the highway may have taken them to exotic adventures and deeds of great import, those wayfarers missed the fun of seeing the town of Perkinston from the seat of my Western Flyer bicycle. As I pedaled along on my paper route, that bicycle was a grand vantage point for a country boy, one which gave me an intimate and friendly view of our neighbors. The experience of seeing and visiting with those neighbors is now a cherished treasure of memories, but at the time it was just having a good time while delivering the news, and making a little spending money, getting to know my paper route.

Things To Do

Before I recount pedaling one more furlong on my paper route, I want to let you know that those of us fortunate enough to live in Perkinston were exposed to unique cultural and social influences during the 1950s.

My first exposure to William Shakespeare, for example, was when as a kid I saw a group of traveling actors who performed The Taming of the Shrew in the college auditorium. One of the actors must have had what we now call a twenty-four hour virus, so his part was played by a stand-in. Though the understudy or stand-in clearly had not memorized his lines, he recited every one of them perfectly. His secret was that every time he spoke he took off his hat. I soon figured out what he was doing: concealed in his fedora was a copy of the playbook. He studiously examined the lining of his hat every time he spoke a line. At the time, I would have preferred watching wrestling on Channel 5, but Shakespeare won.

It seemed that while the entire community believed in the sanctity of marriage as a union between one man and one woman, they also believed in attending "womanless weddings." These outlandish mock ceremonies, usually put on for some worthy cause by a civic club, were carried out in the most flamboyant and humorously slapstick fashion possible, with some prominent local gentleman playing the part of the groom. Likewise, the bride and bridesmaids were also played by local gentlemen (dressed in "drag"). Once, they even persuaded me to play the baby and ride in a wheelbarrow down the aisle, costumed in a diaper! Thenceforth, my preferences along the fundraiser line definitely ran strongly in favor of cakewalks and selling magazine subscriptions.

Every now and again an itinerant brand of bearded basketball players who called themselves the House of David would come to town and make monkeys out of some local Lions club or maybe an actual high school basketball team. If you were at all inclined toward clownish pratfalls and odd shenanigans, these events had a unique appeal about them. I have nothing against basketball. It is a great sport. However, I reckon that nobody in the House of David ever played football or baseball, so they soon lost me.

Perkinston for a while actually had two high schools. One was the Perkinston Agricultural High School, attached to Perkinston Junior College, and the other was just down the street, connected to the Perkinston Elementary School. The latter was called "Little Perk" and the one attached to the junior college was referred to as "Big Perk." Apparently according to Professor Charles Sullivan's <u>History</u>, this dual high school system only lasted from 1949 until September of 1952 when the competing Perkinston Consolidated High School known as "Little Perk" started sending all students to the Perkinston Agricultural High School. I don't know where they got all of the students but I distinctly remember when I was in grammar school seeing Ernie Jordan and some of the high school kids singing, in the old Perk elementary/high school auditorium, a medley of early hits of the 50s. The one that sticks in my mind was, "They try to tell us we're too young."

I started grammar school in 1948 and was like so many other children in and around Perk, privileged to have Gregory Davis as my first grade teacher. She was Mrs. Jim Davis, but she had a boy's name because her daddy wanted a boy, so she got stuck with the name Gregory. She was exquisitely feminine and a wonderful lady in every respect. She introduced us to Dick and Jane and their little sister, who for the longest time as we were learning to read was simply referred to as Baby. Finally at long last we got to the part in the book that told us "Baby" was actually named Sally. As a six year old I remember feeling seriously relieved that she had a real name.

One of the benefits of living on the college campus was that one time I got to meet a magician named L.O. Gunn. He put on a magic show for the student assembly, pulling what seemed like a whole laundry basket full of colorful silk scarves out of his hat, or his cane, and occasionally even producing (from the hat) a rabbit or a dove or a bouquet of flowers.

Movies were shown on the Perk college campus in the auditorium or the "Y" hut by a group of students in the "Projectionists Club." I remember all the Ma and Pa Kettle Films, Hopalong Cassidy, and some Gene Autry standards. Even without popcorn it was lots of fun. Marjorie Main and Percy Kildare were really funny as Ma and Pa Kettle. On special occasions, we would go to the Straub Theatre or the Glo Drive-In in Wiggins.

There was plenty of exposure to the Bible (Gregory Davis was also one of my Sunday school teachers). The Bible, of course, has the greatest stories and literature ever written. As I have already reported, when we sang in chapel in elementary school, Grace Jones and Mrs. Howard Parker also educated us musically. We did not have video games, cell phones, or digital cameras, but we were exposed to lots of good, valuable influences. Before television we had wonderful radio. Somehow (to use Shakespeare's phrase) in my "mind's eye," I could imagine Matt Dillon and Miss Kitty more vividly when I listened to "Gunsmoke" on the radio. Sounds without pictures left your imagination free, and allowed you to experience–first hand–Fibber Magee's closet contents tumbling out when he opened its door. I remember listening to Arthur Godfrey in the morning, Art Linkletter in the afternoon, and kids shows on Saturdays, the latter being sponsored by Buster Brown shoes. Mom listened to daytime shows like "Ma Perkins," "The Romance of Helen Trent" and "Our Gal Sunday," which were sponsored by Oxydol or Halo shampoo or Ivory Soap (thus the origin of the term "soap operas").

The only example nowadays of this old time virtual reality is listening to a ball game on the radio when you are very familiar with the teams and the players who are playing the game.

As I rode about on my Western Flyer bicycle delivering the papers, I was also exposed to a new kind of music. When you have more time, I'll tell you all about it.

A New Sound

When I digressed from telling you about my paperboy adventures, I was about to describe the interesting sights, sounds, aromas and flavors of my peripatetic part time Perkinston vocation. As I would ride past houses and businesses on my trusty Western Flyer, I not only got to see the interesting citizens of our village, but I also sampled the sounds emanating from their radios, smelled their cooking, and if I was lucky maybe even get offered some tasty snack.

I always loved music. As a very little boy when I would ride standing up on the seat tucked in behind my Daddy's right shoulder in our old 1939 Pontiac, he would sing the songs of his generation: "Melancholy Baby," "Alice Blue Gown," and "I'll be down to get you in a taxi, honey..." He could play the violin strictly by ear, since he didn't read music, and he knew even older songs like "Old Dan Tucker," "Turkey in the Straw," and "Way Down Yonder in the Paw Paw Patch." In Church, music was also important. I can still hear Gregory Davis teaching us, "red and yellow black and white, they are precious in his sight; Jesus loves the little children of the world."

From our old Zenith radio, and later, on television, we used to hear a program called "Your Hit Parade" in which the most popular songs of the early 1950s were performed by a Lawrence Welk- type ensemble. Jo Stafford, Giselle Mackenzie, Rosemary Clooney and other regulars would sing about seeing "The Pyramids along the Nile" and basking "in sunlight on a tropic isle, " and how "On Top of Old Smokey" it was "all covered with snow," and how "This old house once held my children" and some song about a guy who spend a lot of time brushing away the "blue-tailed fly."

These were the post-war Eisenhower years, and America was captivated by fads like the hula hoop. Heck, I had one. Consumerism was fueled by the golden age of advertising, and we were good and happy. I even had a pair of beagles named Mike and Ike.

Most homes were not air conditioned, so when I rode my bike past some houses with teenagers, through the window screens I heard a new kind of music, something foreign to anything I'd ever heard on "Your Hit Parade" or "Name That Tune." Wafting across the village was the almost mournful gospel-singer-like sound of "Heartbreak Hotel." It was Elvis's first truly national hit. Other songs I remember from late '55, early '56 were Carl Perkins' "Blue Suede Shoes," Little Richard's "Tutti Frutti", and Chuck Berry's "Maybellene." I was too young to understand all the implications of it, but I knew it was a new kind of music when I heard it.

One memorable song by a group named the Penguins was called "Earth Angel," recorded, I have learned, on the Dootone record label owned by a fellow named Dootsie Williams in Los Angeles. It was recorded in a garage, using pillows to muffle the sound of the drums so the singers could be heard. When they took the rough demo to a DJ to play in Los Angeles, the song became an instant hit. When the Penguins' manager, a guy named Buck Ram, was asked to sign the group to the prominent Mercury Record label, he refused unless they also would agree to sign another, more obscure singing group that he managed. The people at Mercury reluctantly agreed. The bad news was that the Penguins never had another hit record.

The good news was that the obscure group's first song from Mercury was "Only You"– the group was the Platters! "Only You" was recorded in May 1955, and by the fall, with no other songs forthcoming, the Mercury Record people were begging to ask Buck Ram if the Platters had another hit ready. He said they did. They were delighted and asked what it was and when they could hear it. On the spot, Buck Ram came up with the title, "The Great Pretender," then went home and wrote the song, which became one of many hits recorded by the Platters such as "Smoke Gets In Your

Eyes," "I'm Sorry," "My Prayer," and my all-time favorite "Twilight Time."

I liked this new music that I heard floating out from behind window screens, into the yards of houses I passed by on my bicycle, and into my curious teenage ears.

This paper route led me to lots of fun stuff, and I'll share some of it when you have a minute.

Music, Music, Music!

If my preoccupation with the background sounds that gave atmosphere to my 1950s paper route has been emphasized a lot, it was because of a very important fact. Music was the medium that signaled to me and an entire generation of teenagers, incapable of putting our feelings into words, that changes were coming to the placid, post-war years in which we found ourselves coming of age in Stone County, Mississippi, and in other places all across America.

<u>Nothing</u> could prepare us for the turbulent late 60s, 70s and beyond, but the innocent tunes of the 50s helped bridge a significant gap during a time of transition in America – the birth of a brave new world marked by the election of John Fitzgerald Kennedy as President of the United States in 1960. During the campaign, candidate Kennedy said, "The United States looks tired. My campaign for the presidency is founded on the single assumption that the American people are uneasy at the present drift in our national course, that they are disturbed by the relative decline in our vitality and prestige and that they have the will and strength to start the U.S. moving again." The music we heard in the 50s was ahead of that thought – it may have been simple, it may have been different from the smooth Guy Lombardo sounds of the 1940s, it may have put us in touch with our teenage feelings, but above all it was <u>confident!</u> We were in a country that could "Rock Around the Clock." Our girls were "Earth Angels". We were encouraged by The Silhouettes to "Get a Job." We could revel in the simple fact, proclaimed by the Capris, that "There's A Moon Out Tonight." We were robust and healthy and ready when the Del Vikings said "Come Go With Me."

When the Five Satins crooned the all time number one doo wop anthem "In the Still of the Nite," we were confident, content to be ourselves, and we welcomed whatever was around the corner. I believe our innate confidence came from a deeper assurance provided by the place where we grew up and the guidance we received from parents, teachers and friends whose exemplary character we knew to be the bedrock of our home grown values.

I know that the current times in which we find ourselves give many people feelings of anxiety and apprehension. I believe in the American people because many of the same feelings pervaded the nuclear age in which I was growing up, and the truth is that the American people now are greater than ever. We just need to wake up and realize the gifts we have been given. When I listen to the music of the 50s, recalling my days of delivering the news around my hometown, I see the parallels between that time of transition and where we are now. As one of President Kennedy's advisers, Richard Goodwin acutely observed, "from a hundred different centers of energy, belief, frustration, anger, and will, people were beginning to move, gathering determination to force America closer to its own idea of freedom. What a wonderful battle. What a joy to be in the middle of the fight." The music plays on, and I am one paperboy who is persuaded that America's greatest days can lie ahead of us. That is, provided we pull together, banish hate, and realize that our diversity can be our greatest asset. The American Revolution is a process, not an event. We need to realize that the people <u>always</u> should come first, and if they are not being served by our governmental institutions, we need to change those institutions for the benefit of the people because the people are our greatest resource. Because we have the privilege of living in the greatest country in the world we really need to come together to preserve its values. We need to get to know each other and feel the sense of community that living in freedom affords us. We need to listen to the beautiful music of the American soul and spirit.

Sometime we'll have a soda pop and discuss whether The Clovers' "Love Potion No. 9" or The Coasters' "Yakety Yak" had the greater overall sociological and political impact on Perkinston in the 1950s.

A Little Night Music

One time I measured the peregrinations of my paper route on an automobile odometer, and it was fourteen miles. I have to admit that is a very approximate estimate since I probably took a lot of shortcuts on my trusty Western Flyer bicycle as I made my way around town.

From Pal Bonds' service station my route meandered down toward Red Creek where I would deliver papers to Mary Moody, Mr. and Mrs. Jug Miles, and Mattie Varnado. Mrs. Varnado was my teacher in the fourth and fifth grades (which were held in the same classroom.) She could be pretty testy with her wooden ruler and had absolutely no qualms about delivering a rap on the knuckles if you didn't do what she demanded. At the same time, she had a sweet side and would read to us at the end of the school day from Frank Baum's classic, <u>The Wizard of Oz</u>. I was grown up and in college before I ever actually saw the movie version, but when I did, I remembered the story from Mrs. V's class. In my mind, I had seen the yellow brick road long before I heard Judy Garland sing "Over the Rainbow."

After these deliveries, my route took me by Moon Parker's house and down the road where the Sumralls, Cokers and Fores lived. They were and are all good people, and I always enjoyed the sojourn down that shady tree-lined roadway.

I would then deliver a paper to one of those elongated cylindrical <u>Daily Herald</u> metal "paper boxes" that had been mounted onto one of the posts holding the guard rail of the northbound entry road from Highway 49 on the south side of Perkinston. I know that sounds funny to have a paper box just hanging out there on a highway guardrail, but that is where Alf Cole, the well digger, preferred to get his paper. Alf Cole was not the most attractive individual on my route. He was not very clean-shaven, usually had a missing gallus on his overalls, and otherwise resembled either a character out of the Barney Google and Snuffy Smith comic strip or maybe that fellow B.O. Plenty in the L'il Abner comic strip in the funny papers. He smoked cigarettes he rolled using Prince Albert tobacco. I think he drank liquor, too. He was grouchy and ill tempered. He drilled our well when my Dad built our house, and during the process he somehow mistakenly dropped some vital component of equipment down the well casing so that it became irretrievably lost. It was nearly dark, and I can remember hearing some very inventive usage of, shall we say, the Anglo-Saxon side of the English language as he addressed the pipe, the drilling rig, the part dropped down the well, and, indeed, the rest of creation. To this day the incident reminds me of Huck Finn's description of his father's cussing talent:

> "Then the old man got to cussing, and cussed everything and everybody he could think of, and then cussed them all over again to make sure he hadn't skipped any, and after that he polished off with a kind of a general cuss all around, including a considerable parcel of people which he didn't know the names of, and so called them what's-his-name when he got to them, and went right along with his cussing."

***

> "Pap was a-going on so he never noticed where his old limber legs was taking him to, so he went head over heels over the tub of salt pork and barked both his shins, and the rest of his speech was all the hottest kind of language--mostly hove at....The government, though he gave the tub some, too, all along, here and there. He hopped around the cabin considerable, first on one leg and then on the other, holding first one shin and then the other one, and at last he let out with his left foot all of a sudden and fetched the tub a rattling kick. But it warn't good judgment, because that

was the boot that had a couple of his toes leaking out the front of it; so now he raised a howl that fairly made a body's hair raise, and down he went in the dirt, and rolled there, and held his toes; and the cussing he done then laid over anything he had ever done previous. He said so his own self afterwards. He had heard old Sowberry Hagan in his best days, and he said it laid it over him, too; but I reckon that was sort of piling it on, maybe."

I am certainly not comparing Alf Cole to Huck's father, Pap. And what I am about to say next may surprise you. With all his linguistic lapses and other faults, Alf Cole paid his paper bill <u>religiously</u> and with <u>scrupulous punctuality.</u> I learned at a very early age that that particular quality is not to be sneezed at.

You couldn't ask for a better time than delivering the news around Perk. One of these days, I'll tell you more about it.

Where have all the flowers gone?

After delivering papers around Dees store, to the Mertz Bond family and the Polk Evans family, it was time to pedal my trusty Western Flyer up the hill to the Baptist preacher's parsonage, the Bakers, the Mitchells, the D'Olives, Mrs. Bond (Jeanette Rath's Mom), the Krohns, and "Faculty Row"– from Miss Margie Stewart, down the hill, up toward the homes of the Cruthirds, Miss Susie Cooley, Professor and Mrs. Sam Jones, Miss Nora Graves and Miss Kathryn Carey, The J.V. Gammages, and Professor and Mrs. Eugene Clement.

To show you how the times were, I remember Buddy and Irene D'Olive trading for a new Chevrolet just about every year. Buddy worked in the buildings and grounds department at the college, and Irene worked at the college grill. Their 1956 Chevy was pink and charcoal gray, and I thought it was the most beautiful automobile I had ever seen. Elvis had already made pink and black wildly popular when he started buying his clothes at Lansky's in Memphis, where he started wearing his collar turned up like James Dean. Elvis once said, "You can't be a rebel if you grin," and said he had made a study of James Dean. "I've made a study of myself," he said, "and I know why girls, at least young'uns, go for us. We're sullen, we're brooding, we're something of a menace." I reckon I will never be any of those things because Mr. And Mrs D'Olive's Chevrolet, in glorious pink and gray, made me grin, big time.

After skirting the campus, I pedaled my bike all around the dormitories, delivering papers to people in faculty apartments and even to some of the students. I still have my Perk annuals where some of the autographers, for want of something to say, remarked that I was a good paperboy. At each dormitory (except, of course, Harrison Hall, which was the exclusive province of the female students, zealously guarded by Wilma Johnston and where all the males, and certainly paperboys, were forbidden to enter) I dismounted, took the number of papers subscribed for in that particular dorm, and hurried through the halls, slipping the <u>Daily Herald</u> under the recipients' doors.

One of the faculty apartments attached to the old freshman dorm (Huff Hall) was the home of Professor and Mrs. William G. Gregory. He taught math and she taught secretarial science and business. They loved to garden, which was quite a chore for Professor Gregory, as he had had one of his legs amputated when he was young. They fought the battle of the Bermuda grass with uncommon valor, and before my paper route days, when I was just a campus kid, I got into serious trouble for picking one of Mrs. Gregory's prized Amaryllis blossoms. I thought she was going to eat me alive. If Professor Gregory hadn't been such a good fellow, I would have started praying for the Bermuda grass to win, but I couldn't stay on the outs with Mrs. Gregory. She paid her paper bill as faithfully as she tended her garden! (Gregory Memorial Chapel, located on the college campus, is named for Professor Gregory and for the Perk students in the military who made the ultimate sacrifice for our country in World War II).

After Freshman Hall, it was on to deliver the news to Stone Hall, above where the old grill was located on the ground floor before the Wentzell Student Center was built.

It was used as a cafeteria for a while after the postwar "old" cafeteria burned in 1958. (The old grill had previously served as the college cafeteria from 1915 to about 1948, according to Professor Charles Sullivan's book.)

Fahnestock (which was called the Faculty Building) was my next stop, where Mr. and Mrs. Tom Davis (and their pretty daughters Mary Ann and Dorlean) lived. Also on the floor below, the Home Economics teacher, Miss Jananna McInnis, Col. Bob Rivers, the college registrar, Miss Frances Harrell, who taught Modern Languages, and other faculty– I think the Moffett brothers, Guy

D. and Winfred had rooms there. I know this is boring if you didn't know the people, but all of them left lasting influences for the good, and I wish I could tell you about every one of them in detail because every one is a unique story. Miss McInnis, for example, was the sweetest little maiden lady you ever saw. She had big expressive eyes and always seemed busy and concentrated with her work. Colonel Bob Rivers wore striped suits with vests and had a gold chain which festooned his middle and secured his pocket watch; he always had a word of wisdom for me. Frances Harrell was a neat studious sociable maiden lady who was a sharp dresser and had a twinkle in her brown eyes that told you she was a lot of fun. Guy Moffett was the jolly talkative easygoing type; his brother Winfred was quiet, studious, fastidious, polite and amiable. All of these people paid their bill right on time. Perk had always had dedicated and gifted teachers.

In one of Walt Whitman's poems these lines appear:

"I wish I could translate the hints about the dead young men and women,
And the hints about old men and mothers, and the offspring taken soon out of their laps.
What do you think has become of the young and old men?
And what do you think has become of the women and children?
They are alive and well somewhere,
The smallest sprout shows there is really no death,
And if ever there was it led forward life, and does not wait at the end to arrest it,
And ceased the moment life appeared.
All goes onward and outward, nothing collapses,
And to die is different from what anyone supposed, and luckier."

But let us not get into philosophy; like Whitman, "I resist anything better than my own diversity,

Breathe the air but leave plenty after me,

And am not stuck up, and am in my place." (which is delivering papers in Perkinston, Mississippi–remind me to tell you about it.)

Likely Heroes

In the winter time when the days began getting shorter I had to hurry after school to pick up my papers so I could deliver them and get home before dark. I had a pair of coveralls to wear over my school clothes on cold days.

One segment of my route wound down toward Cleo Barnes, Delbert Greene, the Guy Evans family, and by the old football field to the Colan McMurphy family. From that leg of my route, I pedaled to the north side of the railroad tracks and delivered Monk Jordan's paper.

Mr. Jordan was a fine person, in my book. I was friends with his sons George and Cotton and really with the entire family. As Garrison Keillor always says on the radio show the Prairie Home Companion, "The women were strong, and the men were good looking." (Except in the Jordan family it was the other way around.) I just remember them to have been good kids. There are many stories about Monk Jordan, most of them probably apocryphal, because he had a speech impediment. As he was a painter at the college, having to put up with the mischievous Elmer "Sadie" Lee on a daily basis, there is no telling what is the truth and what is not.

Boyce Holleman, the great attorney, who was sometimes known to varnish the truth with considerable embellishment, used to tell a story about Monk Jordan that if it isn't true, it ought to be because it is a good story.

The story goes that Monk, allegedly uninsured at the time, had been involved in a fender bender automobile accident right after the safety responsibility law was enacted. While Mississippi did not have a mandatory auto insurance law, once you were in an accident you had to file a report and show that you had obtained insurance.

To hear Boyce tell it, when the guys in the college maintenance shop heard about Monk's mishap, they started in to ragging him about how, without insurance, he would unquestionably lose his driver's license and his license plate, and maybe even his car! It was allegedly a Studebaker, but Boyce may have said that just because the word "Studebaker" sounded good. As his idle fellow workmen kept talking the direst consequences, Monk, who was painting the ceiling, never bothered to respond. The more they teased, the more unconcerned Monk seemed to be. He just kept on painting.

Finally, exasperated, one of these playfully pestering co-workers said "Monk, ain't you the least bit worried?"

"Nope," a cool, collected Monk replied, "they ain't taking my license or my tag or my car!"

The wags asked in puzzlement, "Why not?"

"Cause, I'm going to see Boyce Holleman, by gum."

"Monk, what makes you think Boyce Holleman is going to help you?"

"Because I voted for him, by gum."

"Well, that ain't nothing, cause all of us voted for him— that don't mean nothing!" (Vigorous nods of agreement among all the peanut gallery.)

"But I voted for him on a jury, by gum!"

Case closed. Boyce used to tell that story, and while it might have made Boyce look good, to me Monk Jordan was the hero in it – 1. He knew the importance of the jury system; 2. He served as a juror when called, the essence of good citizenship; 3. I knew Monk Jordan, and knew he raised a good family, and let me tell you he was always on time with his paper bill! (Boyce always spoke respectfully of Monk Jordan – Cliff Holleman, Boyce's father, also had a speech impediment.)

Perkinston in the 1950s had some really good citizens whose descendants have a lot to live up to and emulate. Sometime, if you're not on jury duty, I'll tell you about some of them.

P.O.E.M.

Since both my Dad and Mom were school teachers, we were always taught to place great importance on the value of a good education. As the humorist Kin Hubbard once said, "I guess from what I hear that most of the school teachers get about three months vacation every year so that they can earn some clothes to wear while they teach." He also said "If money didn't talk, you'd never know some folks were around." Teachers are the exception to that rule because, certainly in my life, and in the lives of most people I know, their actions spoke loudly; they made an indelible impression that lives on and continues touching me.

I know I have extolled the virtues of our teachers at Perk before, but they deserve additional extolling. I delivered their newspapers and sat in their classrooms, and in turn they gave their knowledge and personalities and care to me and my classmates in those wonderful coming-of-age years in the late 1950s.

Garrison Keillor jokingly refers to the POEM organization: the Professional Organization of English Majors. Well, I majored in English because of an abundance of inspiration from some wonderful teachers who taught me, most importantly, to love the subject.

We had a dear little lady named Miss Elizabeth Selby who introduced us to literature – the Puritans of Massachusetts and William Byrd of Virginia, and the great American poets. Later, in college I was fortunate enough to be taught by Miss Nora Graves, a formidable and exacting scholar who demanded the best from us. Miss Wanda Lynn Bond, brand new to teaching, beautiful and brilliant, tamed our rowdy highschool behavior and turned our minds to Shakespeare.

And English teacher Helen Murphy tried to expose us to the beauty of art, literature and culture in our little corner of the world.

One exquisite, neat, beautiful and charmingly inspirational teacher who in fact inspired me to major in English and thereby enjoy the dividends of reading and writing throughout my lifetime was one of my "mostest" favorites – Miss Sydney Alexander. She is a wonderful person, and as a teacher was just a "trip to Paris." She made literature come alive, and in the face of every natural rebellion from intellect inherent to high schoolers with raging hormones that has marked all periods of history known to man, she connected us with some of the true classics and made them unforgettable. She was "Our Miss Brooks" with glamour, and displayed eloquence of thought and language by example, neat and sweet. She was teaching <u>Beowulf</u> to our vacant minds one day and really getting into the primeval savagery of the Old English hero epic. Miss Alexander was so correct and schoolteacher-loveable that as she was reading of the Monster Grendel's mother coming to avenge his death, I just couldn't resist a sophomoric interjection. (The term <u>sophomore</u> comes from a combination of the Greek words "wise" and "ass," or "fool").

Sydney had the passage where Grendel's mother clinches the hero Beowulf in a mortal deathlock with gnashing teeth and terrible countenance, and having them face to face in the cadences of that greatest of Anglo Saxon epic poems, Sydney paused for appropriate dramatic effect.

It was obvious in this tense passage that something was going to happen between Beowulf and the hydra headed monster.

As the monster's foul hot breath enveloped Beowulf's visage, in the tensest of moments in the midst of their mortal struggle, I blurted out for all to hear, "Kiss me baby!" It broke up the class and while I doubt that I will ever be forgiven, Sydney will always be my inspiration as she turned me on to the love of words and stories and the beauty of the classics.

Some time I'll tell you how much literature means to me because of great teachers.

Summertime

Summertime in Perkinston was when we were allowed to go barefoot and roam the woods around Red Creek. Our house was next door to the Berry family, and Jack Berry was the one nearest in age to me. Having been schooled in gun safety by our fathers, we never shot anybody's eye out with our Daisy BB guns. But I know now in my heart that our mothers always must have said a special prayer about it, and that is what protected us. We also made popguns that were tubes of hollowed out wood. Using a plunger, also of wood, we could shoot a chinaberry pretty accurately. We also used winter huckleberry or some other good wood to make bows and arrows.

Because we always had dogs (and sometimes cats) we were not bothered too much by snakes, but occasionally we would see one. Usually it was a black snake or a garter snake or just a common green snake, but on one occasion I remember my Mom killing a real live coral snake. The rule on those poisonous pests: Red or yellow, kill a fellow!

One day Jack Berry and my brother David and I were patrolling the homestead with our bows and arrows when we came upon a ground rattler, as the pygmy rattlesnake is popularly called. Since we were equidistant from each of our respective houses, a small dilemma arose. If we went back to get the classic southern weapon of choice against the snake, the garden hoe, the snake might escape. Since everyone of us was barefoot, sticking together and not separating our forces also seemed to be a prudent idea. We were three freckled faced, barefoot boys pondering our situation to the tune of the snake's alarming rattle.

In the end Jack stepped up to save the day. He drew back his bow and with a homemade wooden arrow which we had sharpened and notched with a pocket knife from a winter huckleberry stick, he shot that snake clean through the middle, pinning him to the ground without any hope of escape. Wriggle and rattle as he might, that snake was a goner. I think Jack and David watched the snake while I fetched adult help and the garden hoe for the final coup.

We were at a family reunion picnic once, down in Handsboro, when as a child I witnessed why the king snake is really the king of snakes. One of them had coiled itself around a ground rattler and proceeded to squeeze him to death and literally swallow him whole.

One time I saw a Giant Indigo snake, which I am told by my brother David is as ferocious to rattlesnakes and other reptiles as king snakes are to smaller prey. They are not poisonous and if you leave them alone, they will not bother you. Instead of being a constrictor like a king snake, the indigo snake immobilizes food with its powerful jaws. He is actually a beautiful indigo color with red-orange tinges around his throat. Since he grows to be over eight feet long in adulthood, the indigo snake is fearless, which has made them endangered to the point of being protected by law. The one I saw was resting by a mud puddle, and when I passed by, giving him as wide a berth as possible, he just flicked his tongue at me and never moved.

Most of these barefoot summer adventures happened before I graduated to become a responsible paperboy. You may be assured that when I was pedaling around on my Western Flyer bicycle, I always wore shoes.

The poet John Greenleaf Whittier said it best:

> Oh for boyhood's time of June,
> Crowding years in one brief moon,
> When all things I heard or saw
> Me, their master, waited for.
> I was rich in flowers and trees,
> Humming birds and honeybees.

***

> Ah! That thou shouldst know thy joy
> Ere it passes, barefoot boy!

    Perkinston wasn't exactly New York City, but I wouldn't swap our private swimming hole on Red Creek for all of Times Square. Let's visit on the subject sometimes, and I'll tell you about that sugary sandy shore and those rippling restful waters, clear and cool.

Swimming and Other Pastimes

I remember one day pedaling my trusty Western Flyer bicycle by someone's house and hearing the song "White Silver Sands" floating out to greet me. I think it might have been the better version by "Brother" Dave Gardner instead of the cheesy Pat Boone rendition. It made me think about the beautiful white sands on the beaches of Red Creek.

To grow up in Perk was to be familiar with Red Creek pretty much on a daily basis during the summer. We went swimming every day if it wasn't raining, and since our property bordered the creek, we had our own private swimming hole.

The public beach and community swimming venue was beside the old Red Creek bridge. This ancient rusty steel structure was down by Casa Hatten's place on the old gravel road to Wiggins, just downstream from the railroad trestle. It was where everyone went swimming, and some of the adventurous souls would jump or dive from the bridge into the cold deep creek waters.

While there wasn't an organized lifeguard system, people looked out for you. My feet slipped out from under me one day and I remember somebody's strong hand lifting me up to safety. It was Edward Ray Coker, and I still appreciate it. Swimming in a creek that has a current is tricky business, and you always need a buddy to look out for you.

We were mostly innocent in our summertime pursuits, and in those in which purloining watermelons could have been involved, the applicable statute of limitations has run out long ago. I would never admit to having been on a watermelon-napping escapade on a moonlight night in July. I would categorically deny that George and Cotton Jordan and Gene and Stevie Daniels and Timmy Sumrall and Maxie Fountain could have been involved in any such venture. You would never get me to say that taking two watermelons from a field on a moonlight night, letting them cool in the creek's waters as we went swimming in the moonlight, and then eating the sweet prizes of our nefarious labors was even the least bit fun. As to any further discussion of this subject I solemnly invoke the rights afforded under the Fifth Amendment to the United States Constitution.

Any adventures we may have had of the watermelon or sugar cane variety, while very edgy to us, were really pretty innocent, especially when compared to some of the things we read about today. John Keats observed that "heard melodies are sweet, but those <u>unheard</u> are sweeter," and in the mystique of the forbidden fruit imagination combined with intrigue made certain watermelons very sweet indeed.

Growing up in Perkinston was like a colorful ribbon, full of adventure. Someday I'll tell you how it still ties me to those times.

Sunday Dinner

My Mom was a wonderful cook. She grew up on a farm in the Lloyd Star community which is on State Highway 550 west of Brookhaven, Mississippi. She had six brothers and one sister and learned to cook on a wood stove from my Grandmother, Ma Durr and the various expert cooks who assisted Ma Durr in the house.

Everyone said my Grandfather, Willis Monroe Durr, was an excellent farmer. He passed away before I was born, but everyone in the family said he was an unusually hard worker who treated all his tenant farmers with fairness and honesty. My Mom said that there were as many black folks as there were white folks at his funeral. I wish I could have known him; I certainly enjoyed playing as a youngster around the old farmhouse and barn and garden and fields he had worked so hard to build. After his death, Ma Durr kept right on running the farm, and always prepared meals when I was visiting her as though all her children were still at home. So her kitchen was a good laboratory in which my Mom could learn her future cooking skills.

My Mom was one of the sweetest people in the world. She went off to high school, boarding at Copiah-Lincoln Agricultural High School. Then after she finished high school, she packed her trunk and boarded the train for Columbus, Mississippi, and a college education at the Mississippi State College for Women. Mom had gumption.

She majored in Home Economics which was a tough major because it required, in addition to all the domestic skills, lots of science courses and a liberal arts background also. She turned out to be a science teacher who gave students her sense of wonder about God's universe, and it was while on her first job at Home School at Big Level in Stone

County that she met my Dad. He was a young teacher at Perkinston. It was during the Great Depression. They had been invited separately to a potluck supper put on by some of the young teachers, and somehow they wound up washing the dishes together afterwards.

I remember wonderful Sunday dinners, usually consisting of fried chicken with all the trimmings – biscuits, peas, mustard greens, mashed potatoes or rice, and usually some very tasty dessert. Sometimes she would cook chicken and dumplings – woo honey! Mom would also cook great cornbread in an iron skillet. She was just a naturally born good cook.

Often my paternal grandparents, Adam and Sadie Blackwell, whom we grandchildren called Pa and Dee, would come for Sunday dinner. We called the midday meal "dinner," and it was indeed the big meal of the day. My Grandfather always praised Mom's fried chicken, which was definitely his favorite. She also could broil a great steak, bake delectable hams, and made fantastic casserole dishes. No TV dinners for us! I am getting hungry just telling about it. To quote the Psalmist: "Man did eat angels' food." Yum!

We had good conversation after Dad said the blessing.

One Sunday, after my Grandfather and I had each set records for going back for "seconds" and "thirds," my Grandmother recited (at least in part) the following very descriptive limerick. It certainly described us to a T!

> "A wonderful bird is the pelican.
> His bill will hold more than his belican.
> He can take in his beak
> Food enough for a week,
> But I'm darned if I see how
> the helican."

We had to laugh – even though our beaks were full!

Don't get me started on how good Mom's holiday meals were – I had to pedal my Western Flyer extra hard to recover from that bon-bon bonanza!

Wood Choppers

My Dad was deeply affected by the Great Depression, an era that spelled economic ruin for most people from 1929 to the time of World War II (1941-1945). When I say he was loathe to spend money, you can believe it. He had a strong conviction that prevented him from incurring any kind of debt and the rock solid discipline to live within his means. He would have agreed fevently with Mr. Micawber in Charles Dickens' <u>David Copperfield:</u>

> "Annual income twenty pounds,
> annual expenditure nineteen
> nineteen six, result happiness.
> Annual income twenty pounds,
> annual expenditure twenty pounds
> ought and six, result misery."

He also had the valuable tried and true experience of having been a career school master when it came to raising boys. My younger brother David and I had plenty to keep us busy on the homestead because Dad made sure of it.

In the spring there was the garden, in the summertime grass mowing, and in the fall we had to rake leaves and get up the wood for the fireplace. At least the wintertime was devoted mostly to hunting!

Although all the seasons were eventful, my favorite time in terms of the chores to be done probably had to be the Fall of the year. As the poet has said, "Some of us call it Autumn, and others call it God."

In the Piney woods we are accused, because we spend our lives among the evergreen pine conifers, of having no traditional seasons of the year. While that accusation is true to some extent, I prefer to believe that those of us who are natives of the Piney woods have more sensitive ways to detect when all the seasons including autumn are coming.

My Grandfather used to say that when you see yellow butterflies flying East, fall is on the way. He and my Dad would say they could feel the fall coming as early as when the "cool nights of August" came to town. They always told me that was the best time to cut down unwanted bushes, because they would "stay cut" and not come back.

The fall of the year in our neck of the woods can be seen by sensitive southerners in the rosy, multicolored hues of the black gum trees, the burnished russet colors of the cypress, and the blazing yellows and oranges of the hickorys and red oaks. You have to be on the lookout for autumn where we live and accept that it does not cascade down upon you as it does in New England, or even in the Mississippi hill country, but it is there, nevertheless, even in our beloved Piney woods.

My Dad chose a place to build our house that was not cleared. It was not "new ground." No matter how you looked at it, it was woods. Other than the temperamental Sears Roebuck push mower that sometimes refused to crank, we owned no mechanical equipment to clear the wilderness. At the time, I never thought much about it because to me only professional loggers and farmers had such treasures as tractors and chainsaws. We, on the other hand, had some shovels, rakes, sling blades, a Kaiser blade, some axes, and a crosscut saw.

My brother David says our Dad had a purpose in providing us with such a plentitude of hardwood trees and bush to cut and with such a limited array of equipment to attack it– it provided us with more than we could possibly do and was an excellent device to keep us out of trouble.

I still have my Dad's old double bit ax; David still has the crosscut saw. Usually when we were cutting firewood, Dad would chop the tree, taking care to notch it in the direction he wanted it to go. He kept his ax and the saw sharp, so when the tree was chopped out, we could use the crosscut saw as necessary to fell it, always yelling "timber" even though we were the only human souls anywhere around it.

After we "limbed" the tree, the crosscut saw and elbow grease made pretty quick work of cutting it into pieces which would properly fit in the fireplace. Then we would start splitting the larger pieces with our axes. Dad carefully instructed us to look for the "wind shakes" in the section of trunk we were splitting because if you could hit that natural fissure in the wood with your ax, the wood naturally would split into sections—halves, quarters, and so on.

I still remember cool mornings when this ceremonious exercise consumed our autumn day, especially when Dad would tease me about my accuracy with a single bit ax. As I was trying to strike the mark, he would say "Son, you chop just like lightning." Then he would smile and pause and affectionately say: "You never strike twice in the same place!"

All of us who grew up around Perk had parents who tried to show us the right mark to strike, and for that we can be eternally grateful. When we're not talking about delivering papers, maybe we can visit on that sometime.

Porch Philosophy

One frequent visitor to our house was Professor Nollie Hickman. His aunt, Miss Alma Hickman was one of the educational pioneers in the State of Mississippi. Nollie was earning his Ph. D. in history. He wrote his dissertation called <u>Mississippi Harvest: Lumbering in the Long Leaf Pine Belt, 1840-1915</u> and later (in 1962) published a book by that name. As he researched material in order to write the dissertation, he interviewed my grandfather Adam Harper Blackwell who had been a logger. As I mentioned, Professor Hickman's maiden Aunt Alma had been one of the founders of what eventually became Mississippi Southern College. Professor Hickman was of course very knowledgeable about the history of the United States. My Dad used to teach a course in American Government and was always interested in history so Dad and Professor Hickman enjoyed many conversations rocking in their rocking chairs on our screened front porch. They solved lots of the world's problems on those pleasant evenings while the ladies were visiting inside the house.

I liked Professor Hickman and felt very welcome as I listened with interest to him and my Dad. One reason I felt I knew him well was because when his son Wade was about to be born, Mom and Dad drove the Hickmans to the hospital in Hattiesburg. I was a little boy, and a wide-eyed passenger on that drama filled journey in that car. Mrs. Hickman was in the throes of labor, and I can still hear Nollie telling my Dad to "Step on it Leonard – drive faster! We were in our old 1949 Chevrolet. Although the experience was kind of scary, I knew everything would turn out all right. Mr. and Mrs. Walter Haley had chauffeured my Mom, with my Dad and me, to the same hospital when my brother David was born. My Dad didn't have to tell Mr. Haley to drive fast – the year was 1948, and we were in Professor Haley's new Packard straight eight sedan, and it fairly lapped up the miles at ninety miles an hour as Haley gleefully roared us up toward Hattiesburg. Now that was an exciting ride! For those of us born too late for midwives and too early for a hospital in Wiggins, all I can say is thank goodness for fast cars!

At any rate Professor Hickman and my Dad talked on those balmy nights on the porch about the changes that would likely occur in the future in America and throughout the world. They predicted the fall of the Soviet Union and thought the time would come when Communist countries would adopt a system of free enterprise much like those in western democracies.

They talked about the sacrifices made by the founders of our country and how serious it was when on July 4, 1776, each of those founders fixed his signature to The Declaration of Independence, literally pledging his life and fortune and "sacred honor" for the idea of a new free country.

They talked at some length on several occasions about how important the written words of the Constitution are to protect each of us as individuals from oppression by those who would turn over our freedom to the government or to corporate interests. Both of them admired President James Madison of Virginia because at the time the Constitution was adopted he, as a member of the House of Representatives, immediately introduced in Congress the first Ten Amendments to the Constitution, the Bill of Rights. Professor Hickman said that Madison's fellow Virginians would not have agreed to come under control of a Federal government if the Constitution had not immediately been accompanied by our Bill of Rights. Those first Ten Amendments are the words which secure and hold safe our freedom of religion, freedom of speech and press, freedom to assemble peaceably, the right to keep and bear arms, the right each of us has to be brought before a judge if the state levels an accusation at us, the right to a trial by jury, and so on.

Their conversations would turn to deer and turkey hunting, and sometimes be about the old times when loggers like my grandfather used oxen and caralogs to get timber out of the woods. My Dad and Nollie Hickman were good friends.

Professor Nollie Hickman was a fine example to me because he obviously placed a great value on education. I remember that he had some good brothers, Jake and PoBoy Hickman, who were regular old country boys who spoke with the South Mississippi country drawl common to all of us. Nollie also had a pleasant drawl, but he spoke perfect English. One evening he remarked to my Dad, "You know, Leonard, I think one of the best dividends I received from my post-graduate work was learning how to write and speak in correct English." His statement was indelibly emblazoned on the tablet of my young mind that evening as I sat there listening to those two devoted teachers on our screened front porch with the crickets and whip-poor-wills providing the background music on such a soft summer night.

One of the benefits of growing up in Perk was the excellent conversation. We were a talkative village. I like the line in The Maltese Falcon when the Fat Man says to Sam Spade, "Talking's something you can't do judiciously unless you keep in practice." If you ever find the time to listen, I'd like to practice telling you some stories about my Perk paper route.

Shopping on Pine Street

Man cannot live by bread alone– on Saturdays it was time to take a break from the paper route and go with the family up to Wiggins. Although it was only five miles away, Wiggins was a much more bustling place than the sleepy, peaceful community of Perkinston.

I always looked forward to haircut day down at Hick's barbershop. It was owned by Otis Hickman, and was named Hickman's Barbershop, but everybody just called it Hick's because they called Otis Hickman Hick. Since I was a respectful southern boy, I called him "Mr. Hick." Otis Hickman, Carlo Breland and occasionally Bithel Price manned the barber chairs, and it was a place for lively conversation. Blaylock's barbershop was also a good visiting place.

The barbers were glad to give us "flat-top" haircuts, and after James Dean and Elvis became popular, they would even leave the sides long for "ducktails." Hick's and Carlo's conversation ran toward sports, hunting and fishing. Bithel Price had opinions about every known subject, and could discuss them all at length.

People don't take the time to talk like they used to do. It seems that all the "time saving" cell phones, computers, and other modern devices do not really leave us time to visit. In the 1950s visiting was a robust art. I realize now that I probably had the opportunity to know some world class visitors as I was growing up in Perk.

Probably the top three female talkers I had the pleasure of knowing were Edna Gammage(Mrs. J.V. Gammage), Berta Patton (Mrs. Charles Patton) and Word Guild (Mrs. George Guild). Some ladies today think they are talkers, but none of them could hold a candle to Mrs. Gammage, Mrs. Patton and Mrs. Guild. If you had ever put the three of them in a room together, you would have had to bring blankets and food and water because they would still be talking. They were all lovely people and very interested in seeing young people do well. As world class talkers they were a veritable trifecta of conversational champions. Believe me when I tell you that each of those fine ladies had the gift of gab, and they gave freely of it to any listening ears.

As to men talkers, I would have to give it to the barber, Bithel Price, the store proprietor Gene Dees, and, of course, to the lawyer, Boyce Holleman.

Mr. Price kept the banter going continuously when he was lowering your ears by giving you a haircut. Sometimes, when he considered the point he was making not to be sinking in properly, he would just stop cutting your hair and come around in front of you so he could put his argument to you eyeball to eyeball. He was such a good talker that when the preacher ran a little short on his sermon he would simply call on Mr. Price to dismiss the congregation by an appropriate oblation, and Bithel was always happy to oblige and take us on out to the end of the hour. For sheer longevity of parley, I would put Bithel Price up there with the best there ever was.

Gene Dees was more of an all day type talker. He kept a running conversation going with everyone who came into Dees Store in Perk. He had a wide ranging intellect, was full of fun, and made everyone feel like they were doing more than just shopping–they were visiting!

As for Boyce Holleman there has never been anyone to match him in conversational versatility, joke telling, and brilliance in such a wide range of topics. He took astronomy at Ole Miss before law school, and his mind was certainly universal in scope. I cannot commit to the printed word his story of the itinerant organ grinder's monkey which undertook to fight a well known Wiggins bulldog, (and won the fight, straddling the poor pooch facing backward, using a pencil to attack the hapless bulldog's rear end) but it is a classic.

Pine Street was a fun trip on a Saturday. Shopping at Yeager's, Bufkin's, a trip to Mr. Watts' Service Station, then down to Pine Street for a haircut at Hick's, then over to see the old maid sisters, Miss Mae and Miss Hontas O'Neal. Miss Hontas' real name was Pocohontas, after the famous Indian princess whose loving intercessions caused her father to spare Captain John Smith's life all those years ago in the colony of Virginia. Miss Mae and Miss Hontas were dear ladies, and no slouches themselves when it came to visiting. I always loved visiting with both of them at their gift shop because they were lots of fun and always had a story. On Pine Street there were two drugstores– Pete Wilson's and Professor Clarence O. Hinton's. Professor Clarence O. Hinton had taught chemistry at Perk years before, and my Dad had been one of his students. His drugstore had a real soda fountain, and the young lady would serve you anything from a banana split to a cherry coke–the perfect end to a mid morning shopping and haircut spree. Down at the end of the street, past the Straub Theatre, were all the Hall brothers stores– groceries to tv sets to automobile tires, they had you covered!

Pine Street will always be a special place to me, for it was there in his office up the hill on the north side of the street that Dr. Joel Simpson uttered three sentences that probably saved my life. I had suffered almost unbearable pain throughout my whole body starting one Thanksgiving day in the early 1950s. I was about eight or nine years old, and as we returned on Sunday to our apartment in Perkinston from the Thanksgiving holiday at my Grandmother Durr's place near Brookhaven, every time the old car would hit a bump my body would be gripped with sharp pains generalized mostly on my left side.

Dad called Dr. Simpson that Sunday afternoon as soon as we arrived home, and on that day of rest, God bless him, he came from his house and met us at his office on Pine Hill. After some painful poking and prodding, the laconic young Doctor Simpson said to my

Dad, "Leonard, I advise you to take your boy up to the hospital in Hattiesburg right away. I will call and tell them you are on the way. I'm certain he has appendicitis."

Dr. Hightower soon was operating on me, and I remember the ether of the anaesthesia and coming to in a hospital room and during the next several days receiving lots of visitors, mainly family members and neighbors and boys who lived in Varsity Hall where our apartment was located at Perkinston Junior College. Dr. Hightower said if I hadn't been sent to the hospital my appendix could have "ruptured" which sounded ominous, and that I could have been very sick and might even have died. I remember that I felt lucky. Forever after, I always had a special respect for Dr. Joel Simpson.

Making a little spending money on the paper route made shopping in Wiggins much more fun. Someday we'll talk more about it.

Ladies

One thing you learn quickly as a paperboy is to be nice to the lady of the house because, more likely than not, she is the one who is going to pay the paper bill. As I have said before, Perkinston had some very dear ladies so it was not such a chore to stay on their good side. Of course, as a teenager I was much more interested in the younger ladies, the daughters of the house, rather than the mothers, and, but for the issue of collecting my paper bill, I suspect most of my attention would have been in their direction.

My brother and I had a wonderful Mom; we were taught at a very early age to respect ladies, young and old, and to act as young gentlemen if we knew what was good for us. In Perkinston in the 1950s there wasn't all that much trouble available to get into if you were a young person. The church and school were the centers of social activity.

Young ladies were just exactly that– they were nice girls who expected and received respect, even from grammar school days. I received my first spanking on the first day of school in the first grade from Gregory Davis for talking in class to Virginia Dare Breland and Joyce Bond so I have to admit that charming young ladies were very interesting to me even at a very early age.

One customer on my route Helen Murphy, who taught English at the college, had three daughters. You can be assured that her paper was delivered promptly and on time every day. Our elementary school principal, J.W. Mitchell, also had daughters, and June was about my age. Mr. Mitchell never missed getting his paper, either.

All these young ladies have been cherished friends down through the years, and as I did not have a sister, such friendships were no doubt a good influence on my early years.

Every time I think of school and some of the sweet and innocent times we had, these lines from John Greenleaf Whittier's poem <u>In School Days</u> come to mind. I can't say that what happened to the narrator of the poem ever actually happened to me, but it easily could have:

> Still sits the school-house by the road,
> A ragged beggar sleeping;
> Around it still the sumachs grow,
> And blackberry-vines are creeping.
>
> Within, the master's desk is seen,
> Deep-scarred by raps official;
> The warping floor, the battered seats,
> The jack-knife's carved initial;
>
> The charcoal frescoes on its wall;
> Its door's worn sill, betraying
> The feet that, creeping slow to school,
> Went storming out to playing!
> Long years ago a winter sun
> Shone over it at setting;
> Lit up its western window-panes,
> And low eaves' icy fretting.
>
> It touched the tangled golden curls,
> And brown eyes full of grieving,
> Of one who still her steps delayed
> When all the school were leaving.
>
> For near it stood the little boy
> Her childish favor singled;
> His cap pulled low upon a face
> Where pride and shame were mingled.

Pushing with restless feet the snow
To right and left, he lingered;---
As restlessly her tiny hands
The blue-checked apron fingered.

He saw her lift her eyes; he felt
The soft hand's light caressing,
And heard the tremble of her voice,
As if a fault confessing.

"I'm sorry that I spelt the word:
I hate to go above you,
Because,"—the brown eyes lower fell,---
"Because, you see, I love you!"

Still memory to a gray-haired man
That sweet child-face is showing.
Dear girl! the grasses on her grave
Have forty years been growing!

He lives to learn, in life's hard school,
How few who pass above him
Lament their triumph and his loss,
Like her, because they love him.

If this book were entitled "Everything I know about the Human Female," it would be a considerably shorter volume. When you opened the cover, I would not speculate as to how brief it really would be: perhaps only one page without a lot of writing. One sentence, maybe. In the 1950s my Mom by her life and her faith made me believe, and nowadays my wife and daughters make me believe on a daily basis that there truly is a God. Who else could make such dear interesting beautiful beings to intrigue and baffle me and pierce my heart and leave me breathless and love me so that I can learn how to give back love and even occasionally love myself?

There were some real Steel Magnolias where I grew up. We'll have a cup of coffee one of these days and I'll tell you all about them.

Pa and Dee

On Sundays, unless they came up to Perk to visit with us, we would load up after lunch which we called dinner and ride down to Saucier to visit my grandparents, Adam and Sadie Blackwell. They lived in a little house on what used to be Highway 49, and the front porch, shaded by an ancient wisteria vine, held a comfortable swing and a couple of rocking chairs. It was there that my grandfather, "Pa", as I called him, smoked his pipe filled with King Bee tobacco.

My grandmother ("Dee" to all the grandchildren, since one of them had trouble saying "Sadie") had come to South Mississippi in 1898 from Jackson, Tennessee, freshly graduated from Ward-Belmont College in Nashville to be a teacher and ready to educate the good people of Success, Mississippi, down in Harrison County. (In 1898 all of Stone County was also still part of Harrison County.) I still have the .32 caliber Smith and Wesson pistol she brought with her to this savage land, a parting gift from her grandfather. She was the principal of a one room school at Success Community ("Reedy Head"), and she soon met and fell hopelessly in love with my grandfather, Adam Harper Blackwell, a good looking logger with coal black hair, pale blue eyes, and a third grade education. By the time I came along his hair was snow white and he had a handsome handlebar mustache.

Adam Harper's Father, Anderson Harper Blackwell, had migrated to Harrison County from Philadelphia, Mississippi, in the 1840s. Soon his father, Morris Blackwell (my great-great grandfather) followed him, and they settled near what is now Morris Hill Baptist Church on Blackwell Farm Road in Harrison County.

My grandfather Adam, born in 1877, logged the yellow pine during the period when Gulfport was the greatest lumber port in the world. He had two teams of oxen– one named Logue and Red, after friends who worked with him, and another named Billy and Teddy, after Presidents William Howard Taft and Theodore Roosevelt. Just as some adults today simply cannot adjust and acclimate to the universe of computers, he was likewise utterly mystified and unable to acclimate to the world of internal combustion engines. As a result, Sadie, for as long as anyone can remember, did all the driving in their Chevrolet automobile, not Adam.

I always loved to visit my grandparents because they had the best magazines to peruse– <u>Life</u> (of course); <u>Look</u>, and <u>Collier's</u>, and sometimes <u>National Geographic</u> and <u>The Saturday Evening Post</u>. They were always ready with a treat which was an RC Cola and some vanilla wafers. I remember their old cream colored GE refrigerator had a funny round refrigerating condenser apparatus on the top of it.

One of the great losses of the modern age, it seems to me, is that we have forgotten what a treasure elderly people really are. They are our civilization's grass roots memory and guides to where we are headed, if we listen to them.

I remember seeing a gruesome piece in <u>Life</u> magazine about the concentration camps in Germany, and I can still hear my grandfather saying "Old Hitler should have read the Bible– you don't mess with God's chosen people." That piece of wisdom translates into much of life, for in my view lots of people qualify as chosen. But, back to the story.

Adam Harper Blackwell was the seventh son of the seventh son. He had many friends of all races who believed that that "double seventh son" distinction imparted special gifts to him. They would come to his front porch in Saucier with their arthritis and their warts and so on, and he would never charge them anything, and they would go away somehow better for the experience. I do not know what he did for them, other than listening--he was always a really good listener– and I do not believe he had any special gifts because if he did, it stands to reason that he would have used them to cure some of <u>his own</u> ailments. But I <u>have</u> witnessed with my own eyes when we would get ready to go fishing, Pa gently approaching a fat wasp nest on the eave of his old garage with his careful hypnotic, gestures massaging the air within six inches of the fully squadroned wasps congregated on the nest and his deft plucking of the nest for fishbait from where it was cemented to the garage, and he never, ever was stung by any of the wasps. So go figure.

There were many mysteries that I witnessed growing up in Perk. When you're feeling superstitious, I'll relate them to you.

Friends

One gentleman my Dad always liked was Lyman Baxter. Lyman, father of Carlie and Carol, was a good storyteller and full of wit and humor. When he would roll up to Gene Dees' store in his truck, you knew there was going to be some entertainment. My father always affectionately referred to him as Lyin'Baxter, except he didn't use the word <u>Baxter</u>, all strictly in good fun because of Lyman's reputation for tall tales.

One afternoon I was there when Lyman rolled up to the store with a load of hogs. Some wag sitting on one of the benches on the Dees store porch baited Mr. Lyman by asking if his cargo was a bunch of "Piney Woods Rooters." That's all it took - - we felt a tall tale coming, and all eyes were on Mr. Lyman.

He paused gravely, took off his hat, eyes twinkling with mischief, and said with all the seriousness of an undertaker: "No, boys, these are not your ordinary piney woods rooters. These here are special hogs. I brought these hogs here all the way down from Baxterville. They are <u>fourth</u> <u>row</u> <u>rooters</u>."

"We never heard of any such thing," said one of the porch codgers. "What's a <u>fourth</u> <u>row</u> <u>rooter</u>?"

Lyman smiled slightly and said, "It's a special kind of hog for special situations. For instance, one of my neighbors always has a fine patch of sweet potatoes. Well, these here hogs are trained up specially to be stationed on one side of the fence and , their snouts are so long that they can just stand there in one place and root plumb through to the <u>fourth</u> <u>row</u> of that patch of potatoes on t' other side of the fence!"

Everybody had a good laugh – and to look at those hogs, I have to tell you, their old noses <u>were</u> long!

Lyman was a good man, and Dad enjoyed his blarney and banter because Dad was also full of it. Dad always claimed his favorite foxhound Bell was so smart that she absolutely and invariably would refuse to hunt on posted land. He said that there were a lot of people who didn't have as much sense as Bell.

Elmer "Sadie" Lee was an electrician at the college, somewhat small of physical stature, a highly intelligent and witty character who always kept a running verbal exchange going with my Dad. As Sadie weighed in at about a hundred pounds soaking wet, my Dad always referred to him as "Fatso Lee." Dad said Sadie carried all manner of pliers and wrenches in his back pocket because if he didn't his behind was so light in weight it would have otherwise just flown off the ground.

Unruffled by such barbs, Sadie always referred to my Dad who was on the heavyset side as "Old Skin-You-Well Blackwell." My Dad's response was always that "it doesn't take much feed to fatten up a thoroughbred."

When Dad was County Superintendent of Education, he always referred to the Sheriff (Ford O'Neal and Woodrow Preston alternated the position for years) as "Mr. Peacemaker." Gene Dees was the "Unofficial Mayor of Perk," (our little village had no real mayor since it was never formally incorporated as a town) and Miss Hontas and Miss Mae O'Neal became "Mary and Martha" or "Priscilla and Aquilla" from the Bible, and Miss Ona Mae Willingham became "Miss Willie Mae Oningham," just for fun. The folks in the Stone County courthouse were not a glum lot.

Louis Armstrong in the song "It's a Wonderful World" sang that when he saw "friends shaking hands, saying 'how do you do?'; They're only saying, 'I love you,' and I think to myself, 'What a wonderful world.'" Old Satchmo's gravel voice gets me every time I hear that song – the friendly, sometimes humorous exchanges of the citizens who lived around Perk communicated what Satchmo was singing about, perfectly.

When you aren't on the run, I want to tell you some stories about some of the other interesting characters I knew as I was growing up in Perk; I bet you will love them.

More on Mr. Lyman

One morning Lyman Baxter and R.D. Bond set about to go to Gulfport to sell their produce. Lyman's truck brakes weren't working so he had been working on them, but the truck was already loaded, and if Lyman and R.D. didn't get to the Coast, the produce would ruin. Facing the immediacy of the situation Lyman said, "Load up, Brother R.D., we are a- goin' to leave workin' on these brakes right here and go ahead on anyways". And so they did.

Mr. Lyman got up to the top of Ten Mile Hill and without brakes the truck started lippity-clipping down Highway 49, roaring down toward Gulfport, when, lo and behold, along came one of Mississippi's finest: a sure enough highway patrolman.

Well, the patrolman seeing Lyman and R.D. flying by, turned on his flashers and his siren and tried to pull Lyman over. Without brakes, however, Lyman had to just dodge the patrolman, and so Lyman's old truck went careening ahead of him and kept flying toward Gulfport.

The patrolman floored it and managed to regain his lead on Lyman but had to get out of the way again as the brakeless Lyman roared around past him once more.

By the third pass, however, Lyman's truck, with a very nervous Brother Bond riding in the suicide seat, was on a climb up another pine covered hill along Highway 49 so Lyman was able to coast to a halt, aided by the ancient law of gravity.

"Don't you know that you could run over somebody driving that way?" asked the perturbed patrolman.

Lyman smiled serenely at the cop, eyes twinkling, and nonchalantly said, "Yes, sir. But don't you know drivin' in front of a fellow's truck is a good way to get run over your own self?"

This response, laden with its flawless logic, thoroughly stumped the poor highway patrolman, so he again tried the offensive. "Just where in this cotton pickin world are the brakes on this old truck?" he asked sharply. "They's back there at my place hanging on the limb of the pecan tree," Lyman softly responded with complete businesslike aplomb. Without his speaking another word, Lyman's mischievous eyes said, "I know I'm in a fix, but I'm laughing at myself here– why not join in?".

The flummoxed patrolman to keep from cracking up threw up his hands and said, "You all better be careful from now on," folded up his ticket book, and walked away chuckling under his breath, his official demeanor a little withered by Mr. Lyman's self deprecatingly humorous candor. You could say Mr. Lyman was lucky, but I would say that good natured patrolman was also lucky to have met Mr. Lyman.

Lyman Baxter used to say that the Stone County Hospital couldn't cure a case of scows in a rag doll.

One time Lyman had to be operated on at the Stone County Hospital. Back in the 50s, whatever the surgery, the doctors cut you from one end to the other. After undergoing his repair and trying his best to recover, Lyman was horrified when two hefty female nurses came into his room saying, "Get up, sir. You are going to have to get to walking."

"There just ain't any way. I can't do it!" Mr. Lyman said. "Yes sir," the larger of the two Florence Nightingales said, "You can do it, and you are right now fixing to do it this very minute!"

Again, Lyman was horrified. He later said, "The two of 'em got me, one on each side, and commenced to get me up and walking, and I got both of 'em down."

"What's the matter with you sir?" said either Myrt or Gert, wheezing and struggling with this ponderous puzzling situation. Said Lyman, "The best I can figure on it is this here: that doctor must have sewed one end of me to the t'other!," This spontaneous bit of Lymanology had the effect of breaking up both nurses, all the staff, and several fellow patients who were in the hall at the time. Lyman had the quality of innocent humor mixed with a keen wit– he could break you up laughing just by saying a sentence.

Take two examples: Lyman's place was adjacent to Byrd Evans' land. During a dry spell, Lyman, while lamenting his own agricultural bad luck and extolling Byrd's good fortune at farming, once dryly remarked, "You could lean a double barreled shotgun on the fence line 'tween Byrd Evans' place and my place and the barrel on his side of the line would fill up with rainwater, and the one on my side would be bone dry!" During that same drought, Lyman was seen walking across his spread carrying an old bucket. A curious neighbor stopped and said, "Lyman, where are you headed?" Not even looking up, Mr. Lyman said in the same tone he would have used to state an obvious fact to a small child, "I'm a-headed over to the pond to water the fish."

Everybody looked forward to seeing Lyman Baxter, whether it was at Dees Store, or when he was carrying his wife to church, or just to pass and visit on the street. He was truly a unique character. Lyman survived to haul many more loads of produce, make many trips to Dees Store, and create many wonderful memories which are cherished by the friends of this wonderful spirit, fine person, and friend to man.

Stars over Ramsay Springs

In the spring of the year, when my Dad was Dean of Men at the college, the YMCA boys would go to Ramsay Springs for a week of camping. The Baggetts and the Lukes who owned and worked the old time resort would welcome us, and there were concrete block cabins where we stayed. I loved it because the Ramsay Springs Resort was like a nature-filled wonderland.

First, it had a great swimming pool fed with sparkling fresh water. Second, it was on Red Creek where there was fishing and picnicking and more swimming. Third, there was this great hotel constructed full of interesting memorabilia and taxidermy (like a stuffed wildcat). Fourth, the hotel dining room served excellent Sunday dinners, the specialty being fried chicken. And fifth, besides the lakes and wide open spaces, there were artesian mineral springs flowing from the ground, each with its own flavor, to cure whatever ailed you. The springs were located under a pavilion surrounded by a nice concrete platform.

I remember the springs pavilion was the venue of a political rally I attended one time, probably during the time my Dad served in county government. Boyce Holleman was the master of ceremonies, and there were acres of people present to hear from the candidates. Our singing Chancery Clerk Hollie T. Bond favored us with a song or two, and the name brand politicians (Sheriff Ford O'Neal, the Tax Assessor Vernon Brown, and maybe Representative Joel Blass) would have followed, along with many others, with speeches. Television, with its insistence on the thirty-second sound bite has ruined politics. At old time political rallies people could listen to a candidate and size him up and make a better informed decision come election day. At the Ramsay Springs rally people had a good time, picnicked, listened to the issues, and had the opportunity to be more engaged as citizens than we ever seem to be these days.

There was an ancient burled knot two or three feet in diameter at the old Ramsay Springs Hotel. It was worn smooth in all its nooks and crevices because I imagine it had been pulled from Red Creek where it was smoothed by the current for eons. I last saw it in the Blow Fly Inn in Gulfport where Mrs. Al Malone, who had purchased one of the Ramsay Spring cabins, had put the curious old treasure on display. Seeing it brought back fond memories of Sundays after church when we would load up and go to Ramsay Springs Hotel for a crispy fried chicken dinner.

A couple of us made a fall float trip from Perkinston to Ramsay Springs one time and camped out on the way. The way Red Creek twists and turns the trip was two and a half days. I remember squirrel hunting during the day and camping at night on the creekbank under a canopy of bright stars. There is nothing quite so indescribably beautiful as the living painting of nature.

"Occasionally in life there are moments of unutterable fulfillment which cannot be completely explained by those symbols called words. Their meanings can only be articulated by the inaudible language of the heart."

These words of Martin Luther King, Jr. could be applied to several of my childhood moments as I was growing up in Perk. I'll try to find the words to tell them to you when you can find the time.

Cars

Whatever we lacked in Perkinston in the 1950s in the way of direct entertainment had subtle compensation in indirect ways, and one of them was the sheer variety of automobiles on Highway 49. The 1950s ushered in the golden age of America's popular love affair with the automobile, and as kids we were interested in anything with wheels.

The students at Perkinston Junior College rarely owned automobiles. I remember Sonny Quave having a carefully maintained Model "A" Ford, but the fact is that there were very few cars on campus.

I wish I still had the second hand 1950 Willys Jeepster convertible my Dad bought for a fishing car – it was really cool. It had gangster style wide white sidewall tires, was black with a white top, and Dad even let me drive it on vacant country roads. I could not believe that he traded it for a Jeep, but there is simply no reforming a confirmed foxhunter, and he wanted something that would take him into the woods where the dogs were running.

On the other end of the spectrum were the luxury cars – R. B. Thomas had a Buick Roadmaster; our Beat Three County Supervisor Billie Parker had a Pontiac (I think it was a 1956 Strato-Streak V8); and Boyce Holleman perennially rode in the latest Oldsmobile 88. I only saw out-of-county Cadillacs cruising by on Highway 49, but Dizzy Dean would sometimes roll into town in a Chrysler Imperial!

My cousin Glendon Johnson drove a Studebaker with a nose as sharp as the beak of a hummingbird (the car, not Glendon). This must have been a popular vehicle for school men because Mr. Shoemake, who was principal at Wiggins, also owned a Studebaker.

When the Ford Motor Company first started manufacturing the Thunderbird in 1955 to provide some competition to Chevrolet's Corvette (first produced in 1953), the tale that spread through Perkinston Agricultural High School was that two Thunderbirds actually met each other on Highway 49 and saluted each other with their horns as they passed. Henry Rath could tell about it. In those days, General Motors had a 45% share of the automobile market in America, with Ford running a close second.

Automobiles in the 1950s were a symbol of confidence in America. It was a dynamic time as our country emerged from the anguished years of wartime privation, and the sense of relief after the Second World War coupled with a sense of unity and changing technology produced a wonderful atmosphere for people who like automobiles. The 1955 Chevrolet was in every sense of the word a brand new type of car. The '55 Chevy had a 4.3 liter, 265 cubic inch V-8 engine with 160 horsepower. When Dinah Shore sang "See The USA in your Chevrolet," people responded and bought nearly two million '55 Chevys.

Combine cool wheels with the birth of rock and roll music, and you can see at once why all of us who were teenagers during these years could have been trouble! Since none of us teenagers in Perkinston actually had keys to these great cars, however, we remained relatively innocent.

I still love to see classic cars from the 1950s. I can remember as though it were yesterday my predecessor paperboy Clyde Hatten delivering our paper to our house on the hill bordering Highway 49 and in the middle of exchanging pleasantries, exclaiming, "There goes a brand new baby blue 1952 Cadillac!" It made us look.

My dad was entirely too conservative, trading our old 1949 Chevy for a 1951 Plymouth that rocked like a boat when it floated down the road. Sometime, when you have a minute, we'll talk about all the cars in Perk; it won't take very long. I promise.

Holiday Song

Reminiscing about Christmas in Perkinston in the 1950s would not be complete without remembering the annual Christmas Choir Concert in Gregory Memorial Chapel. That was when Professor Eugene Clement had the Perk Choir in prime tune, on pitch, and ready to celebrate the holiday season.

Professor Clement, or "Clem," as we affectionately referred to him when he wasn't around, was a consummate professional and perfectionist as those of us fortunate enough to have known him can attest. He felt a calling to his profession in much the same way ministers of the Gospel feel called to preach. Professor Charles Sullivan's great <u>Mississippi Gulf Coast Community College: A History</u> quotes Clem as saying, "I've touched lives as a teacher that I'd never have been able to touch as a preacher." You know, he was right. To those of us who knew him he opened to us a whole new way to appreciate music.

We came from all across the Gulf region– we had sopranos from Wiggins, Lucedale, and Foley, Alabama; altos from Milton, Florida, El Salvador, and Benndale; tenors from Biloxi, Pensacola, Florida, Atmore, and Fairhope, Alabama; bass singers from Perkinston, Vancleave, Flomaton, Alabama and Cantonment, Florida. We were from many small towns across the Southeast, but when Professor Clem tapped his baton and called us to attention, we sang with one voice.

The choir school year started with preparation for the special programs we knew would be scheduled. Eugene Clement was, beneath his cool exterior, deeply sentimental. He almost teared up when he told us we had to be ready to perform at our <u>top best</u> for the Homecoming program, "Because there will be people who will come to hear you who care about this place and their memories of this choir." Enough said– we sang our hearts out for him.

The Christmas concert was fun and very special. The Norman Luboff Choir had some best selling Christmas albums at the time, and we were delighted when Clem obtained some of their standards for us to sing at our evening performance at Gregory Chapel. I'm partial, but to this day I believe Clem had us sounding as good as Luboff's professionals on songs like "Ring Christmas Bells," "Angels We Have Heard on High," and "Jingle Bells." He would make such comical faces when he wanted us to lighten up and sing joyously that we couldn't keep from smiling as we sang.

After the official evening chapel performance we would take a break, bundle up, and Clem would take us strolling around the village of Perkinston, stopping at homes to sing Christmas carols. Sometimes we would be invited in for hot chocolate and Christmas cookies. The only break in the strictly Christmas oriented caroling would occur when we came to L.A. Krohn's home. Clem knew that his wife Myrtis's favorite song was "Tenderly," so in addition to "Deck the Halls," "Silent Night," and "O Little Town of Bethlehem," The Krohns always were feted with "The shore was kissed by sea and mist...Tenderly." It was fun!

Marilyn Lott was in Clem's choir (in <u>later</u> years– she is young!) and as a successor choir director, she carried on the quality tradition of choral music for which the college remains renowned to this day. Delivering papers in Perkinston and singing songs of joy in the Perk Choir are great memories any time of year, and most especially at Christmas time.

Christmas

Christmas in the 1950s was much simpler than the extravagant and hectic spectacle modern society seems to put on us today. We would usually cut our own Christmas tree and Mom would decorate the house with holly and smilax vine, which she called greenbriar. We had stockings that Santa Claus filled with good things to eat–apples and oranges and peppermint candy. Usually as boys our big present was a set of six shooters just like the ones Gene Autry or Roy Rogers or Hopalong Cassidy toted. We also got clothes and other necessaries, but as kids those toy cowboy pistols were what we were waiting for. One year I got my trusty Western Flyer bicycle which served me well on my paper route.

Our family usually went to my maternal grandmother's house west of Brookhaven, Mississippi, to spend the Christmas holiday. Dad would load us up in the '49 Chevrolet and my brother David and I would ask from a point just north of Bond until we rounded the last curve on the gravel road to Grandma's house, "Are we there yet?" My grandmother Eudora Durr was a widow who operated an active farm and lived in a big old ramshackled farm house. She cooked as if all eight of her children were still living at home.

Before Christmas my cousins and my brother and I would build forts from 'Ma Durr's stack of firewood; and riding sticks for horses and using sticks for guns, we would fight battles between the cowboys and the Indians, or we would throw corncob hand grenades at the opponent's fort. We had great fun with no jealousy or envy until Santa Claus would come. Then everyone got his cowboy pistols, and whoever was left with an old fashioned Gene Autry pistol would envy the one with the snappy new Roy Rogers set or the Hopalong Cassidy set or whatever was the latest and best.

The hardest thing about Christmas was deciding what present to buy for Mama. Dad would take us shopping at Yeagers or even down to Gulfport, and my brother and I never knew what she wanted and worried mightily over whatever her possible gift could be. No matter what we got from a bottle of old "Evening in Paris" perfume to a box of handkerchiefs Mom always made us believe she was as delighted to receive it as if it were something specially designed for her by Tiffany's.

Downtown Gulfport was a wonderland of Christmas colors and lights. Sears and Woolworths were magic places, and I can still picture in my mind's eye the electric train set at Sears and the songs being played on the store's loudspeakers– "city sidewalks, busy sidewalks, dressed in holiday style; in the air there's a feeling of Christmas."

At Grandma's house, we always ate plenty of turkey, enjoyed the conversation with the cousins, uncles, and aunts, felt loved by Ma Durr, and returned to Perkinston preoccupied in the back seat of the old Chevy with whatever toys Santa had brought us, constantly inquiring, "Are we there yet?"

Each year I wish for everyone the merriest Christmas ever. Let us always remember why the Christmas holiday is a holy day, and that the birthday we commemorate is that of the greatest gift of all to mankind.

Dees Store

I could write a whole book about Gene Dees' store in Perkinston. It was a rambling old building painted a dusty tan color, festooned with the usual Coca Cola signs, with a welcoming front porch. There you could buy groceries, "dry goods," school supplies, candy bars and comic books. (And just about everything else in the world.) Just going to that store was an adventure because sooner or later everyone in town would drop in and be greeted by the magnetic personality of Gene Dees.

What a character! My Mother said that when she sent my Dad to shop he did more talking with Mr. Gene that he did shopping for groceries. They discussed politics, sports, places they had been and people they had known. It was always interesting to hear them. I loved it because while they were solving the problems of the world, I was by the magazine rack casing, previewing, and sometimes actually reading the comic books!

One summer during high school, I had the opportunity to work for Albert Quave who had been commissioned to assemble the school lockers at the new Vancleave school. We commuted to Vancleave in Mr. Albert's old International pickup truck, and to tell the truth as a fellow to work for he was not the easiest guy in the world. In fact, sometimes he could be, let us say, kind of grouchy. At noon, however, he broke for lunch and we would go to the old store in Vancleave, also owned by a Mr. Dees– Gene Dees' uncle– which was very similar to the Perkinston Dees store, except even more so– same pot bellied stove, same line of merchandise, everything from horse collars to blue jeans to groceries. The main difference was that the Vancleave store had an octagon shaped room in the center, each wall of which was covered with the doors of post office boxes. In Perkinston, we had our own separate post office.

Nobody ever loved Perkinston Junior College more than Gene Dees. He would help deserving students– Karl Hatten, for example, worked there on his way to becoming a doctor. Mr. Gene loved going to football games and was a regular with Boyce Holleman at Ole Miss games. Mostly Gene Dees was about fun and telling stories with his keen wit and wonderful sense of humor.

The Dees store at Perkinston was an institution because it was a gathering place. If you were ever there Miss Ina Vee or Dilly Easterling would wait on you if Gene was in the middle of one of his stories. I thought he was a good businessman because he always made you feel welcome.

The porch had a couple of plain benches where I could take a break from my paper delivering job and have a coke and a pack of peanuts. I could run into just about anybody there, and on the porch Ollie Reeves was, more likely than not, presiding. Sadie Lee might come by, or Leonard Sumrall or Charlie Broadus. The store was the headquarters for plenty of conversation over lots of cokes and root beers and with no small measure of tobacco chewing repartee.

I seem to remember that Mrs. Noll Davis used to come by in her big brown Hudson automobile and have Dilly bring out a case of cokes and place it on the hood of the car. She would then ease up the hill (the Davises lived just up the hill, across from the Perkinston Baptist Church) and I guess the cokes always made it up there to their home safe and sound.

Gene Dees and his wife Mary lived just up the hill, too.

Perkinston was filled with memorable characters, and Gene Dees was one whose generous and affable mark was indelible. Sometime we'll get a coke and a pack of peanuts and discuss the rest of them, when you can spare a minute.

Dogs

I have been thinking of the dogs we had when I was growing up in Perkinston. Everyone ought to own a dog sometime in order to understand why it is that they are called man's best friend.

My first dog was an English Shepherd named Happy. He was tricolored (black, white and some tan) and had a strong herding instinct. If you threw a basketball out into the yard, Happy would try to herd it. I had a great advantage when it came to dogs because my Mom's brother Dr. E.H. Durr in Clinton, Mississippi, was a veterinarian. I called him Uncle Eddie. I always enjoyed visiting his clinic, and on two occasions he gave me a dog to take home to share with my family. I do not know how delighted my parents felt about it, but my brother David and I loved it.

The most memorable dog Uncle Eddie gave to us was a mixed breed part Boxer named Butch. Butch was a wonderful watchdog and came to us fully housebroken. When my Dad was finishing his Master's degree at Southern, Dad would have to take classes in the evening in Hattiesburg and that struggle for education made him have to return home late at night. We were glad to have old Butch because Butch would sleep just inside the back door right by our old Bendix washing machine. Anybody who tried to get in our house would definitely have contended with Butch, and he was formidable.

Butch was very territorial, and if someone came around whose presence he thought was suspect, Butch let the trespasser know it. We had a man who would plow our garden for us in the spring, and one day he came with his mule hitched to his wagon while we were away in Wiggins shopping. When we returned home, Butch had "treed" the poor plowman in his wagon, and from the looks of things when we drove up the driveway, the mule seemed to be trying to climb in there with him. Butch was one superlative, no-nonsense watchdog, and a good friend for a long time.

We owned beagles named Mike and Ike (during the Eisenhower years), and at one time I had a Doberman pinscher named Cindy. She was so fast, she could literally catch a rabbit. There was peace on the old homestead as long as Cindy was around.

My Dad loved to foxhunt so we had a number of foxhounds. My Dad's favorite was a female named Bell who was a very smart Walker and Bluetick foxhound. Her running mates were Blackie (who was really a black and tan coondog that came out of the doghouse and became a foxhound), and Boston, who was part Walker, dark brown and white. We would listen to them run and we had many foxhunting adventures. Every one of the dogs had a distinct personality, and some of them had unusal quirks. To be a black and tan ex-coonhound, for example, Blackie had an unusual preference: she absolutely <u>loved</u> to eat watermelon.

Every young man and young lady needs to know the nonjudgmental friendship and devotion of a good dog. As lawyer George Graham Vest (who later served as a United States Senator from Missouri) once said, "a man's dog stands by him in prosperity and in poverty, in health and in sickness. He will sleep on the cold ground, where the wintry winds blow...if only he can be near his master's side. He will kiss the hand that has no food to offer, he will lick the wounds...that come in encounter with the roughness of the world. He guards the sleep of his pauper master as if he were a prince. When all other friends desert, he remains...and when the last scene of all comes, and death takes the master in its embrace, and his body is laid away in the cold ground, no matter if all other friends pursue their way, there by the graveside will the noble dog be found, his head between his paws, his eyes sad but open in alert watchfulness, faithful and true even to death."

Dogs are special. When I was a paperboy in Perk, I tried to get along with all the dogs on my route. I am proud to say I was never bitten by man nor beast. When you are on break sometime, I'll tell you more about foxhunting.

This picture is of the home of Gregory Davis, my first grade teacher. The John Perkins house, located beyond the east end of Perkins Street in Perkinston, as it appeared on December 14, 2000. The original cabin constructed by John Perkins was contained under the highest middle portion of the roof. In December 2000 the ax strokes made by Perkins in squaring the timbers in the Civil War era were clearly visible in the walls of the back right corner room. The carport at right and the rooms at left were added by the mid-20th century. Photo by Richard Kopp

The Ramsay Springs Hotel was a great place for fried chicken on Sunday. A circa 1920 Ramsay Springs advertising postcard gives the address of the "One-Galus Resort" as Perkinston post office, 20 miles distant. Courtesy of Willie A. Bond.

This fuzzy picture had not changed very much by 1955. This late 1930s view of Perkinston shows (1) the Illinois Central Railroad Depot (originally the Gulf and Ship Island Railroad Depot built about 1900). The building (2) to the right of the depot across old U.S. Highway 49 should be the Bang Store. The Dees General Store (3) is located left of the Depot across Main Street. The large two-story white building (4) north of Dees's Store is the J. L. Power Masonic Lodge. The road crossing the tracks in the foreground is 3rd Street. Straight up the tracks in the far distance (5) the Perkinston viaduct (completed 1937) lofts new U. S. Highway 49 over the tracks.

The Charlie Swetman House (built c. 1892) faces old U.S. Highway 49 in Perkinston in 2000. When I was the paperboy, the Bentley family lived there. The Graves (Swetman) Store was located to the left of this structure. It (the store) eventually became the Perkinston Post Office, where I picked up my newspapers and set off on my paper route.

A circa 1960 view of Dees's General Store established circa 1911 at the corner of 2nd Street and Main Street by Calvin Elias Dees of Ocean Springs. In 1925 "Uncle Cal," as he was called, branched out into the funeral business and purchased an automobile hearse. The store annex, at left in above photo, served as Stone County's first mortuary until Uncle Cal's son, John, built Dees Funeral Home in Wiggins The benches on the front porch provided a good place to visit.

(Left) Calvin Eugene "Gene" Dees, another of Uncle Cal's sons, stands behind the candy counter in Dees's Store circa 1960. With Gene are Miss Ina Vee, John Rogers, and Dilly Easterling. Photograph courtesy of Johnnette Dees. In 1956, Gene Dees became the recipient of Perkinston Junior College's initial Sam Owen Trophy, awarded for outstanding service to the college. He died on April 26, 1965. In 1968 Dees Hall on the Perkinston Campus was named in his honor. In 1966 Elwood Taylor purchased the Dees Store, demolished the old mortuary wing, and constructed Taylor's Store which still stood in 2000 on that site. The new store was completed by Thanksgiving 1966, and the stock from the Dees Store next door was immediately transferred to the new building. The circa 1911 Dees store structure was razed by the end of 1966, its former site becoming the parking lot for Taylor's store.

This white clapboard church held a wonderful congregation. The circa 1910 wooden Perkinston Baptist Church faces 2nd Street. The Doric columns of the circa 1973 brick Perkinston Baptist Church are visible behind the wooden church. The brick church facing Church Street (photo, right) supplanted the old wooden church, but the old wooden church remained standing for some years, serving as the educational department for the new church. The wooden church was moved to the site in the photograph (above, Uriel Wright Plat Block Four, Lot 8) in 1927 from its former location 200 yards to the northwest. The wooden church formerly stood in the north half of the Perkinston Cemetery. There, it had replaced a circa 1898 wooden structure which burned on August 4, 1909, when lightning struck at the beginning of a revival meeting shocking five persons. Throughout the rest of 1909 and into 1910, as the wooden structure in the photograph was being built, the congregation met in the then abandoned former Ten Mile Church building on the north bank of Ten Mile Creek east of the Swetman Store.

The J. L. Power Masonic Lodge. The September 5, 1911, Founders Proposal, which secured the site of the HCAHS for Perkinston, offered free use of "the Perkinston High School Building, which will soon be under construction and will be completed by October 1, 1911, until the agricultural high school is built." Obviously the lodge members wanted the new Harrison County AHS so much that they called their nearly completed lodge hall "the Perkinston High School building" in the document. On December 2, 1911, the lodge members leased the two rooms of the first floor to the trustees of the Perkinston Separate School District. The lease extended for 50 years and the lodge members reserved the right to use the first floor when school was not in session. The lease was terminated in 1922, when the Perkinston Consolidated School was built next door to the lodge. The membership of the lodge razed the grand old historic landmark in 1988 and built a concrete block building across from its site on the south side of the tracks. Classes at the HCAHS were certainly held in Huff Hall in session 1912-1913, and very likely also in one, two, or three other places—the new J. L. Power Masonic Lodge, the old Ten Mile Church-School-Masonic Lodge, and at the Perkinston Baptist Church in the cemetery.

This is the only photograph I could find of the old post office where I picked up my papers. Perkinston postmaster Arl O'Neal stands on the front porch of the Graves (Swetman) Store in 1960. He succeded postmaster Abner Flurry. Photograph courtesy of Arl O'Neal.

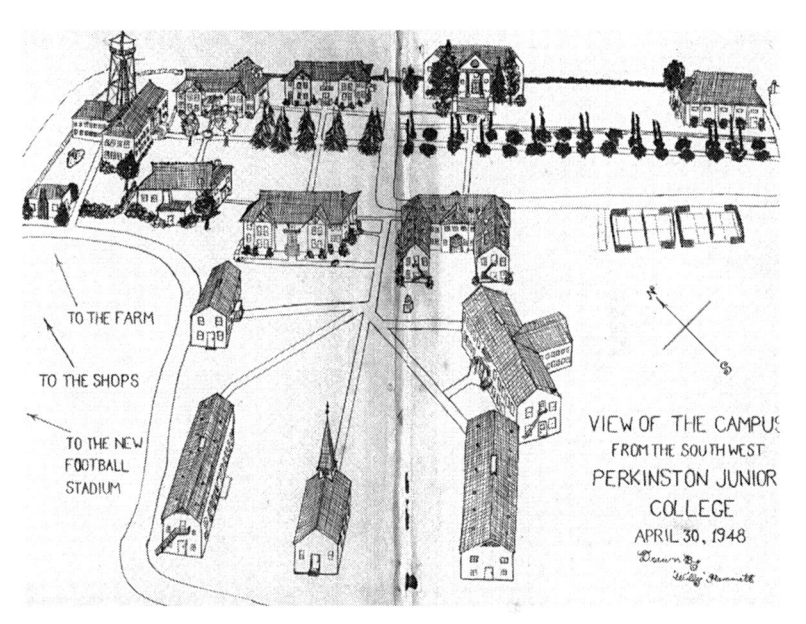

Bobby "Willy" Hammett of Biloxi, a college freshman in session 1947-1948, made this April 30, 1948 drawing, showing the major portion of the campus for the flyleaf of the <u>1948 Perkolator</u>. The drawing does not include the football stadium, shops, and farm buildings to the left, nor does it include the superintendent's home or the Power House and pond. The drawing is fanciful in depicting building detail but the relationship of the structures to one another is well done. The five structures of Military Perk, including the War Memorial Chapel, which was on-site though incomplete, appear at bottom. The Posey Howell Dinner Bell is depicted behind Harrison Hall at its final point of service in that role. Hammett placed no names of buildings on his drawing but their names of 2000 (or names prior to destruction) were added.

This aerial photograph from the 1954 Perkolator taken within a few months of President May's death on July 8, 1953, shows the campus as May left it. The tennis courts were moved and the Wentzell Center was built there. The swimming pool where I earned my lifesaving merit badge, the last facility built in the May era, appears in the Quadrangle between the tennis courts and the Old Gym. The pool, completed in August 1953, is filled but not fenced and the scars of construction still surround it. Most of the other May-era structures are visible as well. The five buildings of Military Perk are visible at left. A. L. May Memorial Stadium is at the top of the photo with the Colmer Building standing complete across the street. Due to the trees, only a portion of the World War II-era vo-tech complex of shops and garages is visible between the Colmer Building and Bennett Hall.

This is the "old" grill as I remember it until 1958. According to the caption of this photograph from the 1952 Perkolator, p.60, the students pictured are "Campusology Majors." This campus grill, which opened in January 1948, was dubbed the Snack Shack by popular vote in February 1952. The Snack Shack was located on the ground floor of Stone Hall and was fashioned from the 1915-1947 dining hall after food service began in the Cafeteria and Classroom Building. The jukebox in the photograph had virtually played out by May 11, 1955. According to the Bulldog Barks of that date: "Students are wondering why something can't be done about the grill jukebox. For some time there was a problem concerned with keeping current hits on the machine. Now we have the songs but on a machine not in condition to play them. After putting money in the juke box, it is necessary for a student to jolt the machine to get proper results from a stuck record, thus losing half the playing time and effect of the song. "We are wondering if it would be possible to have a new juke box in good playing condition which would also carry one hundred recordings instead of the small number our present jukebox holds. Since students spend so much money on the jukebox, aren't we entitled to more music played the way it should be played?"

Choir Director Eugene Clement (right) and Sam Jones take a break in the Cafeteria and Classroom Building in 1952. Clement had been on the job for three years and Jones had just arrived. They still "had it all before them." In his retirement interview in May 1986, Clement created a "word picture" of the 1950s era.

"Those were the days of dress codes and strict social behavior. The young men wore dress pants and shirts--and even ties--to class. The women had to wear dresses or skirts and blouses. Why, the men and women weren't allowed to sit on the benches and hold hands. When the sun went down and the outside lights came on, the women had to go into the dormitory not to come out again that evening."

When an evening choir practice was scheduled, Clement said he would go to the women's dorm, line up the choir members, check them out one by one, and march single file to practice. After practice, they were marched back to the dorm and checked in.

"In fact, the students used to take every other letter except one out of the name Perkinston and they would have P-R-I-S-O-N. And that's almost what it was like in those days when the sun went down."

Clement said that in the earlier days there was no need for a discipline committee. Instructors and dorm supervisors handled their own discipline problems.

"I don't recall what kind of punishment the women had, but the men would have to dig up stumps. There were a lot of big tree stumps on campus. The student was given a shovel and an axe and a certain amount of time to get the stump out of the ground. When you saw a fellow digging a stump, you knew he had done something real bad 'cause that was the most severe punishment one could get--other than being sent home. But one thing for sure, it gave him plenty of time to think about what he had done. Most all disciplinary action was in the form of work."

I loved Professor Clement and Professor Jones – they were tops!

At the January 22, 1964, Board of Trustees meeting, the Board named the academic deans who were to take charge of the three campuses of MGCJC on July 1. (from left) William P. Lipscomb named academic dean of Jefferson Davis Campus, Curtis Davis named academic dean of Jackson County Campus, President J. J. Hayden, and Charles G. Odom named academic dean of Perkinston Campus (replacing Lipscomb). These men were real leaders, and I admired them.

This picture shows your humble Paperboy wielding the "whip" at the 1957 Boy Scouts of America Jamboree held at Valley Forge, Pennsylvania. From left are my fellow scouts Darryl Breazeale, Tom Fowlkes and David Redfield. Photo was probably taken by Wynn Alexander.

On our way to Valley Forge, the Scoutmasters took us on a side trip to Washington, D.C. Here is the Paperboy in a rare moment of reverent silence before the Tomb of the Unknown Soldier at the National Cemetery at Arlington, Virginia.

Your humble Paperboy ready to hop on the Western Flyer bicycle and deliver the Daily Herald to all my fellow townspeople in Perkinston, Mississippi. Photo courtesy of Charles Sullivan, along with all photos and proceeding captions (except for the last two preceding photos) for which the author is very grateful.

This photograph of my parents, Leonard A. Blackwell, Sr. and Myrtis Pearl Durr Blackwell was made in the 1930s. They were two schoolteachers who married in 1933. They were married 44 years. Mom died in 1977, Dad in 1982. They left a legacy of love.

Photograph, circa 1950, of Dad, Mom, my brother David and me. It was probably taken at Perkinston Junior College when we were just back from a day in the country – great memories.

Fashion Statement

It is not that clothes really matter or that there was any kind of apparel contest going on in Perkinston during the 1950s, but whatever happened to be in style, I was one step behind the trend. To a teenager in the 1950s that sort of thing seemed terribly important, but looking back I can see it really wasn't.

Teenagers universally want to fit in and feel part of the acceptable group – growing up years are sensitive in that way! So when I started the ninth grade at Perkinston Agricultural High School, the first thing I noticed was that I was slightly out of costume among my peers.

Now you have to understand that the dress code for boys was blue jeans, white shirts in the hot "short-sleeved" months, and casual jackets in the winter. Sounds simple, but as we had kids from the Coast and out of state metropolitan areas going to our high school as boarding students, subtle differing dress standards marked some of them from those of us who were day students. We would arrive early to school and sit in the breeze way connecting the two parts of the old library and science building (where the high school classes were held) and as a freshman I could observe these differences up close and personal.

The "cool" kids wore Levis; my jeans came from Sears Roebuck. The fashionistas wore penny loafers; I had lace ups that served more as work shoes than grill-hoppers. The young James Deans wore leather jackets with their collars turned up; I had a blue jeans jacket from Old Miz Sears. At least in the socks department, I and my fellow day students were up to date: <u>everyone</u> wore <u>white</u> socks!

I can tell you exactly what I wore the morning of January 25, 1958. That was the day the old cafeteria burned down, and when I arrived that morning to gawk along with everyone else in town, I had on the coveralls and boots that I wore when I had to pedal my trusty Western Flyer bike to deliver papers in bad weather. "Through the rude winds wild lament and the bitter weather," as the song says. On such occasions I also had a plastic raincoat and waterproof cap. When it absolutely stormed, Dad would relent and take me on my route in his car, but during the years I was the Perk Paperboy, I can count those times on one hand. This sounds like one of those "when I was a boy, we had to walk ten miles to school in hip deep snow" rants, but I am really not complaining.

The paper route taught me as the poet James Whitcomb Riley said, "It hain't no use to grumble and complain, It's jest as easy to rejoice; When God sorts out the weather and sends rain, Why, rain's my choice." As I recall, the morning the cafeteria burned down, it was cool and clear.

Thinking back, my fashion anxiety was pretty silly. Some of the cool kids with clothes from the Toggery in Gulfport didn't do any better than others with patches on their jeans (the latter of which would be considered cool today).

In other words, in the immortal phrasing of Willie Dixon's song, as sung by Bo Diddley and a host of others:

> You can't judge an apple by looking at a tree
> You can't judge honey by looking at the bee
> You can't judge a daughter by looking at the mother,
> You can't judge a book by looking at its cover.

***

> You can't judge a fish by looking in the pond
> You can't judge right from looking at the wrong
> You can't judge one by looking at the other
> You can't judge a book by looking at the cover

You get the point. We had plenty of dividends growing up in Perk. To this day most folks I know in Stone County do not judge your insides by looking at your outsides. And looking back, I had a good time pedaling around good old Perk. Good enough to tell about when you can give me a minute or two.

Gentleman and Scholar

One great person who positively influenced my life at Perk was Dean W.P. Lipscomb. He and his wife Tina have always set good examples for young people, and they mean so much to so many of us who labored in the scholarly trenches at Perk in the 50s and early 60s.

Bill Lipscomb served as the Academic Dean at Perk until he assumed the position as the vice president of the Jefferson Davis Junior College Campus on the Coast. Tina was and is his helpmate and was the inspirational sponsor of the Wesley Foundation, the Methodist Student Group at Perk.

Bill is one of the "Greatest Generation", having weathered World War II and having served honorably in post war Austria in the occupation forces. His experience and academic training readied him to be a pragmatic and inspirational leader at Perk and later at Jeff Davis. I got to know Bill up close and personal as his paperboy and later as we traveled together to some professional school meetings that I was allowed to attend representing a scholastic fraternity called Phi Theta Kappa.

The first of these trips was to Memphis, Tennessee, to the Southern Association of Junior Colleges in late Summer, 1960. At the time, I rode the bus and met Dean Lipscomb in Memphis. I remember that on our night off we went to see Kirk Douglas in the movie "Spartacus."

Our other trip was a real adventure because it was in Washington, D.C. at the American Association of College Administrators. We caught the train in Hattiesburg and felt, like in the Johnny Cash song, "rich folks eating on that fancy dining car." We were drinking coffee, but I don't remember us "smoking big cigars." The train's sleeping compartment beds folded down just like in the movies, and when we awoke the next morning, we were in Virginia, heading to D.C.'s Union Station!

We stayed in the famous Shoreham Hotel, one of the great old hotels of America. Dean Lipscomb and I explored all over its grounds and probably saw every nook and cranny while we were there. One evening after a day of business and some sightseeing as we were walking to a late supper through the spacious lobby, we actually saw President John F. Kennedy! The President had come from giving a speech to another convention at the hotel, and I will never forget the magnetic charisma that he carried, shaking hands and greeting the people as he moved across the hotel lobby. It was a time of confidence in America, and I was grateful to be there to see its embodiment in our young and robust President. He was of the Greatest Generation, just like Dean Lipscomb!

Dean Bill Lipscomb is one of the real educational leaders and pioneers who gave Perk and later the Mississippi Gulf Coast Community College the tradition of excellence that is still emblematic of these great institutions. It has been a dividend of my life to know and be inspired by him. Perk was a great place to grow up, because we had the opportunity to come in contact with some wonderful people.

Sometime when you want to share a coke and a pack of peanuts, I'll tell you what advice the Russian soldier gave Major Lipscomb while he was in Austria – it was about an idea the Russian had hatched to get money in a hurry if he ever had the chance to come to America and so he advised Bill Lipscomb to shoot a particular rich person and take all his money. Being a good person, Bill Lipscomb was naturally horrified, but Henry Ford would have put on some extra bodyguards if he had heard the conversation because Ford was the man the Russian advised Bill to shoot.

Losing Your Marbles

Does anybody remember playing marbles in grammar school? I can recall days in the old Perk Elementary school when I <u>literally</u> lost my marbles, and it was deadly serious. Unsupervised playground activities for boys ranged from mumbly peg to tops to marbles. It would be hard to say whether tops or marbles was the more entertaining activity.

In marbles the kids who had a connection with the ball bearing industry seemed to me to have a distinct advantage. They would come to school with a large, shiny steel ball bearing to use for their taw, or shooter marble. Since I had no such industrial alliances, I had to use an ancient blue and white glass taw that I probably inherited from one of my older cousins.

In order to determine who would be the first shooter someone would draw a line in the smooth, flat, bare sandy, area of the playground where everyone always played marbles. We would then "lag" our shooter marbles as close as we could toss them to the line with the closest shooter thus winning the right to shoot first. All of us tried to precisely "taw the line."

By this time for our playing field someone would have drawn two circles on the ground – the larger one approximately six feet in diameter and a smaller one somewhere inside it, about one foot in diameter.

Thank goodness the older boys would usually call "funsies;" otherwise I would have entirely lost my marbles before even learning how to play the game. Maybe we were not supposed to play "for keeps," but sometimes we did. But many of the games were declared at the outset to be just for fun – and it really was fun.

You put the marbles you were staking for a particular game inside the smaller circle, and then the first shooter would knuckle down at some point on the line of the large circle and aim for the stakes. As I recall, it was sort of like shooting pool because if the shooter managed to hit one of the stake marbles and knock it out of the small circle, he got to take another shot.

Sometimes your shooter marble would wind up inside the big circle which made it fair game for any of the other players to take a shot at it. If you were playing for keeps, this could be extremely dicey. You were supposed to be able, if your shooter marble fell victim to a hit in this dire circumstance, to trade two of your regular marbles for it. I do not recall much mayhem resulting over this game so the rules must have been well understood by everyone.

Some of the bigger kids set good examples for us on the playground. One I remember was Roland Mallett. Whenever a bully would start to pick on the little kids, Roland would set the bully straight right quick, and actionably so if necessary. On the other hand, if a group of kids were to gang up on yesterday's bully, Roland would stop that misbehavior just as quickly. Essential fair play is a good thing to learn early, and Roland set a good example.

One day remind me to tell you about my smoking my first cigar behind the old gym and how I got caught, and how the punishment was nothing compared to how sick I got from smoking the cigar. I should have had better sense – but at the time I was just a grammar school kid, too young to be a responsible paper boy.

Boy Scout

When Joel W. Mitchell came to town to be principal of the Perk Elementary School, I confess that the fact that he had beautiful daughters was of much more interest to me than his background in Scouting. Little did I know that he was going to become the Scoutmaster of Perkinston Troop 110, stay on us until we earned our merit badges, take us hiking and camping, and even make it possible for us to go to the 1957 Boy Scout Jamboree in Valley Forge, Pennsylvania.

I had wanted to become a Boy Scout since the time I was in grammar school. My Dad took me to visit camp Towanda, the camp that existed before Camp Tiak was built. The idea of camping out, learning to navigate in a canoe, hiking and learning how to tie esoteric knots was appealing to me. There was a Handbook for Boy Scouts that covered all the rules and had tips on how to build a fire, survive in the wild, tie knots, cook breakfast, and so on.

Besides, our assistant Scoutmaster was Jim Byrd, the old WWI Vet, and he was someone I knew and respected. Our first camping trip was for one night, and we slept on a fine sandbar on the banks of Red Creek. I remember looking up and seeing the Milky Way, and that night there were several dozen shooting stars. Uncle Jim announced that he was going to sleep with his head on the down slope of the creek bank because it would help the circulation of his blood. Everyone lay under blankets and talked back and forth, and it was not until very late, or early, depending on your point of view, that we actually got to sleep.

One weekend Mr. Mitchell took us on a five-mile hike down Red Creek, and we camped overnight at the mouth of Mill Creek.

I remember packing my pack with all the essentials. I remember how good breakfast tasted when it was cooked over an open fire. I remember how cold Mill Creek's waters were where they flowed into Red Creek. Being a Boy Scout suited me just fine.

The hardest merit badge I remember was lifesaving which I took as a course taught at the college swimming pool. We were drilled until we could hardly crawl out of the pool. I remember receiving a certificate at the end of the course which entitled us to the lifesaving merit badge. I haven't had to save anyone's life yet, and I also haven't personally drowned; so far, so good.

The Valley Forge trip was a wonderful opportunity to see the country and to meet Scouts from all over the United States. Wynn Alexander from the troop in Wiggins was a patrol leader, and so was I. This meant we had to make sure all the latrines were dug, all the tents were pitched, and watch out for the eight or ten kids in our respective patrols. By then we had progressed from Tenderfoot to Second and First Class to Star and then to Life Scouts. Kearney Dedeaux, Buddy Patton, Darryl Breazeale, David Redfield, and the Folwkes Boys, Tim and Tommy, were all on the bus with many others. On the way to Valley Forge the bus took us to Washington, D.C., where we toured all the monuments and landmarks and visited the Tomb of the Unknown Solider. We heard an open air concert performed by the Marine Corps Band in an arena on the banks of the Potomac River called The Watergate Arena, long before that name carried other meanings. We went to see a major league baseball game in Philadelphia where the Phillies played the Chicago Cubs, and a boy scout on our bus from Lucedale named Claude Passeau got to sit on the Cubs' bench (his Dad, who served as sheriff of George County had been a star pitcher for the Cubs).

I recommend that every young man and young woman consider the merits of Scouting. It helped me to be a better paper boy, and to aspire to its values has been good for me all my life. Sometime when you want a laugh I'll tell you about how I earned my cooking merit badge.

Buddies

Every boy needs to have buddies. I was fortunate growing up in Perkinston because throughout elementary school and high school and on into adult life I have known some people whose friendships have lasted.

In elementary school Dan O'Neal, Bill Shoemake, Vernon Patton and Herschel K. Rouse were my good friends. Every year or so the schools would consolidate and send us new people from the hinterland. Thus we picked up new friends from McHenry, Saucier, Success, Advance, and so on. Luther Melvin Breland was in one of those migrations and became a buddy. There were many others.

While friends are one of life's greatest blessings, they can also get you into a world of mischief, not as in forcing you at gunpoint to commit some imprudent act, but let's just say they can sometimes be the innocent (or not so innocent) bystanders who handle the stage props that set the scene for your folly.

Since we attended Perkinston <u>Agricultural</u> High School, all boys were required to take two years of instruction in the subject of agriculture. Similarly all the young ladies had to learn home economics. Ed Goff was our high school agriculture teacher - in -chief, and he was a jovial, kind, often frustrated soul who as earnestly tried to educate us about the mysteries of agriculture as those who were trying to escape farm life sought earnestly to avoid learning about it. As classes were held across campus, over by the stadium in the remote vocational-agriculture building and there were no girls around for us to try to impress; an air of jocular familiarity, a rather <u>informal</u> learning environment so to speak, presented itself. I wish

I could say this atmosphere discouraged mischief, but, alas, it did not.

So it was that someone far more familiar with chewing tobacco than I was (or will ever be) suggested that before going into Mr. Goff's one o'clock lecture I might enjoy trying out during the class my very first real chew of tobacco. It seemed to me like a swell idea at the time.

We were seated that spring day for some reason in the classroom where the drafting students usually attended class. That meant we were on high stools instead of our regular school desks. Maybe it was the altitude, but about halfway through the class I began to feel far less enthusiastic about every aspect of this entire chewing tobacco caper. In fact, if I hadn't started to feel kind of queasy, I would have been searching for a place to stash the chew and the spitoon-cup and just forget about the entire business, but there I was so very high up, bellied up to the old drafting table and listening to Mr. Goff's treatise on various bovine infectious diseases that could, if not kept in check, annihilate entire herds of innocent cows. I recall thinking or feeling that what Mr. Goff was describing to us was sort of nauseating even to hear about.

One minute later I was feeling queasier, and the more dire the diseases became, as catalogued by Mr. Goff, the less certain I was of my own health, perched up on that stool.

I will not talk about falling on the floor, white as a sheet, or Mr. Goff's surprised reaction. My strong advice is to avoid lectures on mad cow disease after a big lunch. Oh, and avoid chewing tobacco in such circumstances also.

My friends were very kind to me. They still are. After all, they were friends from Perk who helped me learn about life. One of these days I'll tell you some of our adventures.

Temperamental Mower

There was a time when our temperamental Sears Roebuck push lawnmower that sometimes refused to crank started right up on the first pull, when it wasn't supposed to do it. I'm getting ahead of myself. First, you have to know that to make a purchase of a lawnmower powered by an internal combustion engine was no doubt for my Dad a process of strained inquiry and analysis because he was loathe to spend money. He had probably been looking in the current big-city-telephone-book-sized Sears Roebuck catalog and ruminating over the proposed purchase for quite some time.

Then one has to consider that Dad probably had loaded the family in our old car and traveled all the way to Gulfport to buy the mower from the store which he always referred to as "Old Miz Sears." All I really remember about the purchase of this new shiny red and gray push mower is that when we got home he stowed it in the garage. Before he left for work the next morning, he gave me strict orders not to fool with it until he got home.

You already know that we had great neighbors in Perk. The house just south of us was occupied by the Wilsons, then the Berry Family, then the Cannons. Further south were Mr. and Mrs. Jowann Dedeaux who were dear people. Across the road were the Renicks and the Penley Quave family, all good folks. Penley Quave's son Charles was a little older than I was, and we covered every inch of the woods and played and fished and hunted in and around Red Creek together. Charles had an inquisitive streak about him and was interested in new things and in particular in how things work generally. They could have named him Curious Charles and they would not have missed the mark at all.

Well, later that day while Dad was still working in the Courthouse in Wiggins (where the County Superintendent of Education's office was located) Charles came by the house for a routine visit. Naturally, when the talk got around to things such as, well, new lawnmowers, I felt the need to exhibit to him our latest family purchase, admonishing him strictly (because I knew how he was about such things) not under any circumstances to touch, tamper with, or otherwise come into contact with the new Sears Roebuck lawnmower.

Having a superabundant fascination with the novelty of a machine that would crank right up and mow your grass, and probably wanting to share that enthusiasm with me, Charles assured me that he knew about things such as lawnmowers and not to worry because all you had to do to make it start, (not that he would ever consider such a thing in the face of my admonitions) was to place your foot <u>here</u> on the side of the mower and then grab the handle conveniently fixed to the pull cord <u>there</u>, and that while he was not going to actually start the engine, just pull on the rope <u>one time</u>, and then, well, to my extreme horror, the engine immediately <u>cranked right up</u>!

What flashed through my mind next was an instantaneous technicolor picture with sound of my Dad remarking, almost as an afterthought, when he left for work that morning that the reason. I was not to fool with the mower until he returned home was that it might not have any oil in it so it wouldn't be a good idea to crank it in that condition because such a thing could damage the engine. I have just described my concern about problem number two.

I have been entirely too wordy in telling the first half of this story, and I want to finish it properly. I promise I'll tell you about problem number one the very next time I see you.

Problem Number One

The last time we visited I recounted how the Temperamental Sears Roebuck Push Mower that sometimes refused to crank behaved on its maiden voyage by cranking right up when my friend Charles Quave accidently? unexpectedly? impulsively? pulled only once on the starter rope. There it was clattering away like a very loud sewing machine, if sewing machines were powered with Briggs and Stratton engines, which quickly put in my mind Problem Number One: how to turn off that machine.

The assured expertise that Charles brandished on the way into this caper seemed suddenly to vanish into thin air. All I could do was listen to that clattering engine and imagine the dire consequences toward which it was clattering me because I was going to be responsible when the cloud of impending doom fell.

I soon learned that while Charles might well be the state expert in the field of unanticipated engine starting, when it came to turning the engine off, he was cluelessly worse than the greenest and most unmechanical novice. However, I have to give him high marks for quick assessment and handling by trial and error every visible knob, handle, button, switch and lever on the machine to try to shut it off. He even at one point, as we were jumping desperately around this incessantly clattering, seemingly gremlin-possessed little engine seized on the notion that the spark plug would be a good place to grab, but all that futile gesture did was give Charles an unnecessary jolt of electricity to fire up his already unnerved state of high anxiety and further deepen my worrisome gloom.

All of this took about fifteen or twenty seconds when I suddenly realized the unthinkably inevitable– it was time to stop jumping around and go tell Mom about this whole deal. She did not even try to parse the mechanical Rubik's Cube of how to shut down the engine. She simply went to the telephone and made the call to my Dad. My felonies were compounded when I realized the gravity of the situation, for in those days a call from Perkinston to Wiggins on our party-line phones was <u>long distance</u>!

In what at once seemed like the geologic slow-down of time and also in nothing flat, in a cloud of dust up our driveway came my Dad. He sized up the situation immediately, found the cut off switch to the mower (which must have been disguised while we were searching for it) and turned off the engine. He then said gravely, "We'll have to let the motor cool down so I can check to see if it has any oil." That phrase concentrated my mind wonderfully.

After what seemed to be about an hour, but was probably just a few minutes during which my Mom had some sweet iced tea ready and my dad seemed surprisingly unmenacing and in fact almost good-humored about the situation, it was time to check the oil.

H.L. Hunt's preacher never prayed more fervently for oil to be discovered than I prayed for oil that day. When I say that I wanted oil to be in that engine, you can bet that every Bible verse I had ever memorized was marshaled in my mind to make it happen.

When Dad unscrewed the oil plug and that beautiful viscous amber liquid overflowed its cell, I was as happy as I would have been if we had just struck the Pistol Ridge oil field.

Charles and I had to bear a lot of kidding in the days to come, and Dad didn't have to scold either one of us. We learned a lot of lessons that day.

I mowed lots of grass with the Temperamental Sears Roebuck Push Mower in the years to come, and a couple of jobs, when I tell you about them, will probably make you laugh.

Lawn Mower Lesson

Dearly beloved, this tale is another in the saga of the Temperamental Sears Roebuck Lawn Mower that sometimes refused to crank. I learned a valuable lesson using it one time on a job in Perk, a lesson that has stayed with me even until now.

It was a particularly hot summer and I had scrounged up lawn mowing jobs around town to make a few dollars. It was the summer before I inherited the paper route, so I would have been about twelve years old.

The worst jobs were those with bitterweeds. Those tough, smelly plants were no fun to cut, and their stench stuck to everything. I don't know if you have ever had a glass of milk from a cow that has grazed on bitterweeds, but if you have, then you know what I'm talking about.

I had mowed the cemetery, and a couple of private jobs came up, and of course I didn't get paid anything for mowing our yard there at the homestead. So I was aggressively drumming up business.

I can't say that I hadn't been warned. The old couple who said they had a job for me were known around town as, well, stingy people. I didn't know enough to refuse employment, however, and at the appointed time they specified, which was 7:30 A.M., I showed up with the Trusty Temperamental Sears Roebuck Lawn Mower. And it, on that day, cranked up just fine.

The job, when I saw what it was, should have made me run away and leave the mower and the people and forswear any other lawn mowing employment forever. It wasn't a lawn to mow, it was a whole lot to clear covered with weeds, bitter, sweet and otherwise, some of which were higher than my head.

By 4:30 P.M. in the hottest part of the afternoon the lawn mower stopped working. Shortly thereafter, so did I. The lot was cleared, and there was not a sprig or stubble anywhere on it higher than two inches. I was bone tired, dusty, and tuckered out completely.

My employers, who had grimaced when I took thirty minutes to eat the peanut butter and jelly sandwich my mom had fixed for my lunch and drank a couple of glasses of water, came forward for the reckoning.

"How much do I owe you?" my master asked, squinting into the setting sun's rays.

I had never had to ponder that question before. All my other jobs had been for an understood price. So for a moment I hesitated like a deer in the headlights.

"Well sir, you can just pay me what you think the job was worth," was my trusting, hopeful reply. (After all, I had been raised to believe in the Golden Rule.)

My dusty, sticky, bedraggled and bone tired jaw dropped when the old man pulled out his coin purse (this was definitely not going well) and counted out six quarters into my equally dusty, sticky, bone-tired hand.

"I may use you again," he said with a rather dismissive inflection and turned and went inside his house.

I learned a lesson that day more valuable than the lawn mower or even the price of the lot I had just labored to make so neatly cleared of weeds: unless I valued what I did, and unless I communicated that value of an honest day's work to the one who was to pay for my services, I was on the losing end of the lawn mowing dance. That lesson is Biblical as our Lord said the greatest commandment is to love the Lord with all your hearts, souls and minds and love your neighbor <u>as yourself</u>. But you have to learn: placing a fair value on yourself is part of that great equation.

Once I started delivering papers, I cut no more grass for stingy people, and I have never done a job since without a fair understanding in advance regarding my compensation.

Going on Vacation

The first family vacation trip I remember was to the mountains of North Carolina. My Dad loaded us up in The 1949 Chevrolet, and we left very early in the morning on our family adventure. We had with us Bill Gilliland, who operated the mechanic shop for the county's fleet of school busses, as we were taking him to High Point, North Carolina, where he was to pick up a brand new school bus for the county schools and drive it back to Stone County.

Traveling in the 1950s was much more personal in the sense that you got to see and pass right through the downtown areas of every town along the way. Before interstate highways that is how everybody traveled. While one of the greatest achievements of President Eisenhower's administration was construction of the interstate highway system, we had far more time than we had money, so getting the neighborhood flavor of every town just seemed like a natural part of the adventure we experienced on the road.

We wound our way up through Meridian, Mississippi, on to Tuscaloosa, Alabama, then Bessemer, then big Birmingham. By this time the hills were growing into little mountains and my eyes were growing wider by the mile as I had never seen mountains before. We spent the night just south of Chattanooga, Tennessee, and I remember that we were singing "Chattanooga Choo Choo" as we checked into the "Tourist Court" and how excited I was about being on my first real vacation.

The next morning was crisp and cool (this would have been around late August or early September of 1952) and Dad said we were going to take a side trip up Lookout Mountain. The place held historical significance in our family as one of our ancestors had fought for the South in the Battle of the Clouds, but I confess that I was far more interested in seeing the much advertised wonders of Rock City.

All the way up the highway to Chattanooga, when you weren't deciphering the sequential Burma-Share rhyming signs, what every birdhouse, every shed and most especially every barn roof proclaimed was the imperative message, "See Rock City." You had better believe that I was ready to see it.

We wound our way up beautiful Lookout Mountain with all its quaint souvenir shops selling freshly pressed apple cider and real Indian tomahawks and plates with all the sights of Chattanooga emblazoned on their china faces, and far down below I could see the Tennessee River tracing the footprint of a giant Indian mocassin. Finally we arrived at the gate of Rock City.

As I have previously recounted, as a boy growing up in Perkinston before Disneyland was built, before color television, and certainly before anyone had ever heard or even thought of a thing called a "video game", I was pretty easily amused. Rock City did not disappoint me.

I remember walking out on that porch that was literally a ledge in the side of the mountain and being told I was seeing seven states. I remember how we laughed when my Dad carefully edged through "Fat Man's Squeeze". I remember the walls of quartz crystals that looked like diamonds and precious jewels to me. I remember running ahead on the trail to see what wonder was around the next corner. That thrill of new discovery is a good feeling at any age.

After we saw all of Rock City, we stopped for a cold glass of apple cider at one of the little stands on the road leading to the top of the mountain; there we found in the battlefield park real cannons and historic markers telling about the battle that happened there between country boys who wore grey and blue uniforms so many years ago. My Dad told about our ancestor Captain Nick Blackwell and how he had holes in his uniform cap because he would run it up on the end of a stick to taunt The Yankees and how they would blast away at it. Uncle Nick came out of that war without a scratch. He was one of the extremely lucky ones.

The next day we motored further on toward North Carolina. Next time I'll tell you what I heard during the night when they put my brother and me to bed on the sleeping porch at the place where we were staying.

Vacation Memories II

When we last were visiting I was telling about our first family vacation- a trip to North Carolina. We had seen Rock City and were winding our way through East Tennessee. Along the roads that wound through the Tennessee and North Carolina mountains we would see <u>real</u> Indians selling their handicrafts from little stands, usually advertised with hand-lettered signs.

We were headed to Waynesville, North Carolina, where Mr. and Mrs. W.D. Smith operated a big old ramshackled 1920s-style boarding house. Mr. Smith had taught woodworking at Perk and his wife, Mrs. Lessie Smith, had operated a similar boarding house in Long Beach, Mississippi. For a while, they would spend the summers at their North Carolina boarding house and the winters at their Mississippi Gulf Coast boarding house. Eventually they sold the one in Long Beach and lived full time in North Carolina.

Their boarding house was right out of a Thomas Wolfe novel or that Moss Hart play, <u>You Can't Take it With You</u>. They served breakfast and dinner to their regular boarders and kept a couple of rooms available to rent to travelers like us. Mrs. Smith was a Spring Byington -like, upbeat type, archetypal boarding house headmistress, and she ran a tight ship. Her two old maid sisters, Bernice and Velma, lived in the place and both of them were school teachers. Since we had known all of them at Perk, we felt very welcome.

The night we arrived a cold front had pushed through the mountains. Mrs. Smith had a room for my parents and one for Mr. Gilliland who was traveling with us, but after those rooms were taken, there were no vacancies. This meant my brother David and

I had to sleep on the screened sleeping porch which ran all the way across the back of the house.

Mrs. Smith put us in the big old bed and started piling on quilts and blankets until we were as warm as two pieces of toast. The temperature eased down into the forties, but we were snug and warm. She had told us that the cool weather would make the apples ready to pick and that in the morning we could do some apple-picking in her backyard.

Sure enough, as we lay there in that fresh, cold, exhilarating autumn night, the apples started falling around us in the yard to let us know it was time to pick them. We would hear a "plop!" and know one of those apples had just been released from the grasp of the mother tree. It wasn't very long before David and I fell fast asleep, thinking of how good those apples would be. (And of course, they were!)

Bernice and Velma took me to school with them the next day, and I had the opportunity to meet some of the kids from rural North Carolina. They were just like my friends back home in Mississippi in so many ways. They wore similar clothes, they were friendly, they had the same country and small village ways about them.

We had a memorable vacation and I had plenty to tell my friends and family back home!

Little Fellows, Eccentrics and Acceptance

Perkinston had a kindergarten long before such educational advances appeared in most of the state. My mom operated it in the den of our house. I do not remember everyone who attended, but I know Larry Krohn and I believe Burnis Breland and Mal White and cousin Douglas Blackwell may have been some of her pupils. There was a little long and low table with some little chairs, and I guess they must have learned something besides sliding down the steep hill by our driveway on the thick pinestraw. (I know they learned that particular activity was fun.)

Mom was a Cub Scout den mother with Mrs. Randall Dedeaux, whose Christian name was Zettie. Her son Edwin Dedeaux was one of their cub scouts.

I remember on one occasion just before Easter Mom was hosting an Easter egg hunt, probably for one of the grades at Perkinston Elementary school where I was a student. What was remarkable about that wonderful spring day was what we found while hunting for the Easter eggs. In a little bowl-like cache in the ground, all lined with very soft fur, there were five baby rabbits. Mom made us replace the leaves and straw that were camouflaging that private rabbit home and told us not to play with those baby rabbits because the mother might sense our strange meddling and abandon her babies. I remember worrying about it, but we dutifully complied.

There was an eccentric gentleman who lived behind our place, on past Jim Davis' pear orchard. I would have to pass his little cabin on the trail through the woods that was my short cut to walk to school. His name was Charlie Howell. He lived with, but also apart from, his family. His son and daughter-in-law had a house just behind the Perk Elementary school gym, but Charlie lived in his little cabin. He would engage in conversation and was not as reclusively eccentric as some people said he was (He was still pretty eccentric). One day I encountered him cussing at a group of yaupon bushes as he cut them down. He was close to eighty years old, I reckon, and he would climb a ladder and jump over into the top of one of the bushes and ride it down to the ground, and then he would cut it at the base before the bush straightened itself up again. The problem was that you never knew in what kind of mood you would find him, and he could be pretty grouchy, so most of the kids steered clear of his place when they would use the short cut through the woods.

Looking back, I suspect Mr. Charlie may have been a more benign fellow than the hermit he was sometimes pictured to be-- sort of like the Boo Radley character in <u>To Kill a Mockingbird</u>. I never knew him to do anyone any harm, and I suspect his eccentricity was born of some very tragic circumstance.

I suppose in our little village we accepted eccentricity and even insanity, and certainly death. They were just part of life. I can recall in our little town in that very dry county that we had a sad character who was the town drunk. The poor fellow drank Dr. Tichenor's antiseptic. We were told to avoid him.

On the other hand, a guy named Drew Hasty had come home from World War II with a nervous condition. He lived with his parents in a cottage just to the south and east of Gregory Chapel, and the Hastys were good customers on my paper route. Drew was always a perfect gentleman around me, and his folks were as sweet a couple as you would ever want to know. They treated their son with love and kindness and people respected his dignity.

One other person I remember with compassion was a young man named Johnny who was visiting with a married couple who were college teachers and who were very nice people. He was an extremely religious fellow and was always recruiting those of us who were younger than he was to participate in the regular youth programs in the church. He was always quoting Bible verses, and while he seemed overly prudish, nobody could argue with his sincerity. We started noticing little half inch strips of paper, each about five or six inches long, with Bible verses typewritten on them, thumb tacked or taped to the trees and bushes around the college campus. Sure enough, it was nephew Johnny who had put them there. Nobody could understand just why he was being the anonymous phantom midnight Bible verse posting person, but everyone just smiled and accepted it. The little strips of paper seemed to multiply almost as fast as love bugs do in their season, but everyone kept accepting what by now was regarded as a definite eccentricity. Hints were laid that Johnny was becoming somewhat overzealous since you could not swing a cat anywhere on the campus without hitting a typewritten Bible verse on a little strip of paper taped or tacked onto something.

One day my Dad came in shaking his head and said sorrowfully, "You all know that nice young fellow Johnny? Well, his uncle and aunt are having to send him back to Georgia because he has suffered a nervous breakdown. He read the Bible to the point that he became convinced that the Lord did not mean for people to wear clothes so he was running around naked as a jaybird today putting his Bible verses on all the trees and bushes and buildings. It is really sad; this afternoon his uncle and aunt are taking him back to his home." I reckon Johnny skipped the part where Adam and Eve became the first fashion plates.

And that was that – I remember that nobody laughed or cried. We accepted that Johnny was ill and everyone still thought highly of his uncle and aunt because everyone knew that they were fine people. This first brush with mental illness for me was to have it presented as a malady, not as a sin.

Come to think of it, I recall the old folks referring to certain bad conduct in the same way. "Has so-and-so been treating you ill?" they would ask. This perspective, that intentional mistreatment from someone is a sign of illness borne by the one doing the mistreating, is pretty fundamental as a mechanism to deal with life on life's terms in any decade.

As to acceptance of death, we all know that the traditional southern funeral is a visiting of friends. I believe that is why they refer to the wake as the "visitation." We are visiting with one another and remembering the deceased. In the 1950s death was not as sanitized and removed and commercialized as it sometimes can be these days. I recall spending the night in a relative's house with the coffin in the living room, where friends had come by during the previous evening and where the funeral director in the hearse would come to carry it the next morning to the church for the funeral and then to the cemetery.

Lots of people were born at home, lived and loved at home, and died at home. Death was just part of life, and we were thankful that we had a faith that even overcame that final chapter.

Growing up in Perkinston we learned that you can't judge anyone's insides by what you see on the outside, and that whatever you might lose by learning the truth about any given subject probably wasn't worth having in the first place.

Some day when we have more time, we can philosophize about it.

The Grill

One of the fondest memories of my high school years was the old Perk Grill, located on the campus on the ground floor of Stone Hall. When I arrived at Perkinston Agricultural High School in 1955, it was the socializing center, complete with a long serving counter, tables and chairs, the ever present jukebox, and ping-pong tables for our recreational pleasure. This was where the cool kids passed their time between classes.

I believe Roy Strickland worked at The Old Grill as a student, and Mary Price (Mrs. Bithel Price) and Irene D'Olive (Mrs. Buddy D'Olive) were the main managers. The Grill in Stone Hall (which I call the old Grill) remained in place until the New Grill opened down the hill in the new gym, eventually called The Wentzell Center. It was fortunate that the new Grill was constructed when it was because when the college cafeteria burned down in January, 1958, The Old Grill then became the cafeteria until a new cafeteria could be built. Mrs. Price and Mrs. D'Olive just moved on down the hill when the new Grill opened and kept on serving us those good hamburgers.

Some of the songs I remember on the jukebox (as I was waiting my turn for a game of ping-pong) were Tennessee Ernie Ford's "Sixteen Tons", "It's all in The Game" by Tommy Edwards, and "Young Love" by Sonny James. One day I was sitting in the new Grill with Harold "Monk" Rouse and Ronald Laz Bond killing time waiting for my next class when two good looking coeds came through the door, both of them wearing pink sweaters. Of course Monk then had to go over to the jukebox and play "Pink Sweater Angel." Up until then I thought his only talent was playing ping-pong.

Both the old Grill and the new Grill had television sets. I remember watching the now famous fifth game of The 1956 World Series on the television set in the old Grill. The Yankees were playing The Brooklyn Dodgers, and after losing the 1955 series to Brooklyn they were wanting some payback. I was pulling for Brooklyn, even though I was more a fan of the St. Louis Cardinals and the New York Giants. The reason everyone remembers that fifth game of the 56 series is because that is the one in which the Yankee pitcher Don Larsen pitched a perfect game– twenty-seven batters up and twenty-seven batters down in nine innings. The announcer told us history was being made, and that day it was futile to pull for the bums from Brooklyn– Larsen was flawless.

The Perk Grills were a great place to hang out, listen to a little music, and talk with friends. I guess we were making good memories without realizing it, which is the way life ought to be.

I realize how lucky I was to have grown up in a place like Perk during the 50s. Whatever ping-pong skills I mastered (which were meager compared to Dale Carson, Monk Rouse, John Loper and many others), I certainly owe to the old Perk Grill.

When you have the time, we'll discuss the jukebox songs in more careful detail.

Courthouse Days

When my Dad served as County Superintendent of Education, sometimes he would let me go with him to his office. It was probably when Mom was at her W.M.U. meeting.

The Stone County Courthouse was an interesting place. As I have mentioned, there were some great Stone County lawyers: Joel Blass, Boyce Holleman and Bob Newton, just to name three of them. There were also Sheriff's deputies and other county officials and sometimes court was even in session.

Hollie T. Bond was the Chancery Clerk, and his efficient office manager, who later was elected Chancery Clerk in her own right, was Miss Ona Mae Willingham. (Dad used to tease her by calling her "Willie Mae Oningham"), and she was a real lady and a true Steel Magnolia. Speck Moore was Circuit Clerk, later to be succeeded by Helen Rae Preston.

In those days the Sheriff was limited by law to serve one term at a time. In other words, the sheriff couldn't succeed himself after serving his four year term. Ford O'Neal and his "brother-in-law" Woodrow Preston (Helen Rae Preston's husband) had the perfect solution to that constitutional limitation; Ford could be sheriff for one term, then Woodrow would be sheriff for the next term. Then after four years they would switch and Ford would serve again. Both of them were good lawmen. I can still remember my Dad greeting whichever one he happened to meet by saying "Good Morning, Mr. Peacemaker."

Helen Hatten (Mrs. Arlan Hatten) was my Dad's able secretary, and she was always a perfect and impeccable Southern Lady.

Joel Blass represented the School Board and also served as a Legislator, representing Stone County in the state House of Representatives. When the United States Supreme Court decided in <u>Brown vs. The Board of Education of Topeka, Kansas</u> that people of all races were entitled under the United States Constitution to attend the same schools, the decision provoked great resistance in the South where public schools had been segregated by race.

It seems strange now that there were two separate school systems in Mississippi: one for white people and one for black people. The poorest state in The Union was attempting to support two separate redundant parallel school systems. No wonder we were 48th in the nation in education (Alaska and Hawaii were not states at that time.)

What was even stranger was one reaction to the <u>Brown v. Board of Education</u> decision that swept through the Mississippi Legislature. The way to avoid integrating the schools, said some of the racially prejudiced firebrands in the all-white legislature, was very simple: we will, they said, just simply amend the State Constitution and ABOLISH the entire public school system.

To his credit, Joel Blass courageously led the fight to save public education in Mississippi. There were debates held around the state pitting those favoring doing away with the public schools against Joel Blass and other defenders of public education. I am proud that my Dad assisted Mr. Blass in the effort to save public education.

Blass took many stands in the Legislature against proposed laws that he knew to be both immoral and unconstitutional. He incurred the wrath of the powerful segregationist group, the Citizens Council which sent one of its members to Stone County to defeat Blass in the 1955 election. While many of his Stone County constituents disagreed with Blass' positions, his good character and record of service to his community overcame their prejudice, and it is a story worth telling.

The Citizens Council guys would post scurrilous handbills on all the telephone poles around town falsely denigrating Joel Blass' record. One of them was known to accuse Blass with actually having friends who were colored people and saying at the end of his diatribe of accusations against this distinguished lawyer, "You know, I don't hold it against him personally, but he is a Catholic." In short, they pulled out every dirty trick possible to defeat Joel Blass, even to claiming that he was such an outcast in Jackson as a legislator that he could not gain admittance into any state office. "They slam the door in his face," they alleged.

The negative campaign began to backfire. One morning, when Blass was walking down Pine Hill after going to the Post Office, a friendly old gentleman caught up with him and as he was passing by whispered out of the corner of his mouth, "All this stuff against you has just gone too far, Mr. Blass. My family is with you." Blass just knew that the odds were that the voters could not overlook their prejudices, and so he prepared his family for the worst. "We will go down to the courthouse to watch the election returns come in but you all need to be prepared. Daddy's going to lose the election," he told his wife and daughters.

To the credit of the voters of Stone County who knew what a good person Joel Blass was, they fooled Mr. Blass; they re-elected him in 1955 by casting 70% of their votes in his favor!

He went on to become a distinguished, outstanding attorney and a Justice of the Mississippi Supreme Court.

I think one of his great accomplishments was the contribution he made in saving public education. In the course of the debates the segregationists who wanted to abolish the public schools were made to look hateful and foolish, and the real powers in the Legislature, who actually were in control, were led to say publicly that they would not under any circumstances allow the public schools to be abolished. It was a case where speaking truth to power really worked.

All of us who attended public schools remember a favorite teacher who made us toe the line. We revere their dedication and honor them for the difference they made in our lives. Thank goodness for the efforts of men like Joel Blass.

The reactionary firebrands lost their fight to abolish every public school in Mississippi.

We should be proud that from Stone County the leadership emerged which helped save the public schools in Mississippi. The 1950s were a happy time, but there were fractious times, too. I am proud of Joel Blass' efforts on behalf of public education. And if you are reading this, you can thank a public school teacher.

I learned a lot on my paper route, but I surely am glad there was a public school I could attend, too.

Saving the Library

As the new year proceeds I am reminded of some of the county leaders I had the opportunity to know when I was growing up in the 1950s. Stone County has a rich history in local government and has produced some wonderful public servants.

Since my Dad served for a while as County Superintendent of Education and had an office in the courthouse, when he let me come with him I got to know many of the county officials. The old courthouse is a treasure in many ways, not the least of which are the memories and stories it can tell about the people who made Stone County great.

The Bond who was the perennial Chancery Clerk in those days wasn't an expert hunter of raccoons, but he was a heck of a singer; his name was Hollie T. Bond.

John Dees was president of The Board of Supervisors, and Ott Bond was the able supervisor for the District that includes the Big Level.

The flamboyant lawyer Boyce Holleman used to tell the story of one instance in which The Board of Supervisors caused an uproar among several of the Steel Magnolias, and John Dees and Ott Bond were the ones who calmed the storm.

Holleman said that as he was beginning his term as the young District Attorney he was in the courthouse one day when he saw Miss Alma Hickman striding in with a determined look, clearly in a state of high dudgeon. Now Miss Alma was one of the founders of what is now the University of Southern Mississippi, a great supporter of public education, and a very formidable Stone County lady. She obviously was as mad as a wet hen that day, and Holleman soon discovered that it was because the Board of Supervisors in a moment of fiscal and cultural misjudgement had just voted to do away with the Stone County public library. The only supervisors who objected to this folly were Bond and Dees, but they were outvoted 3-2. Miss Alma wanted funding restored, and she wanted immediate action.

After much pondering and several behind the scene contacts with Mr. Dees and Mr. Bond, Holleman got their commitment to make the motion and second to restore the funding for the library. Both of them told Holleman it probably was a hopeless situation; however, they agreed to bring up the issue at the next Board meeting.

Meanwhile, Holleman called each of the "aginers" and told them the issue was coming up, and that he would appreciate their reconsideration on behalf of the Library. After each of them solemnly protested there was no way he could change his vote because the County just didn't have the money, Holleman had a ready answer. (Remember, Boyce Holleman was a young D.A. at the time.)

Holleman: "Well, I appreciate your position about the county supervisors not being able to find the funds for the library, and I'm going to see if I can't help you out because I know that deep down you really support having a library for the little children and a place where the good citizens of Stone County can go and check out books and everything, so here is what I'm going to do– we have a Grand Jury coming up next week, and I'll have somebody from the State Auditor's office come down, and you all can come over and bring all the county books, and if we all work together going over those books, there may be some way we can help to find the money for the library."

The following Monday John Dees made the motion to restore the library funding, Ott Bond seconded the motion, and it was successfully passed by a unanimous vote.

It was a privilege being able to know the fine people who were elected officials in Stone County as I was growing up. Sometime we'll go by the courthouse and have some coffee and talk about them.

Tolerance

At the top of the hill at Perkinston Junior College there used to be the Library building. It was where the Agricultural High School was headquartered, where Professor K.P. Faust taught chemistry, where Miss Jananna McInnis taught home economics, and where Mr. Humphrey Olsen manned the library.

I liked Mr. Olsen– for one thing, he was helpful to me when I wanted to check out a book, even when I was just a kid on campus, not yet a real student of the school.

He edited a magazine called <u>The Snowy Egret</u>, named for the beautiful white waterfowl that sometime haunt the riverine marshlands and swamps along The Coast. I remember seeing copies of the magazine when I stopped by the checkout desk, and he helpfully assured me that I wanted to check out <u>The Virginian</u>, the western novel by Owen Wister, not <u>The Virginians</u>, the sophisticated English novel by William Makepeace Thackeray.

As I have mentioned, the 1950s were in many ways an idyllic time; certainly it was a great time to be a kid growing up in Perk. In other ways it was a fractious time; The Cold War was brand new, and national leaders emerged who capitalized on our fear of Communism just as some southern politicians kept getting elected by instilling in people the fear of the unknown, waving the flag and yelling "segregation forever!" One such national political demagogue was Senator Joseph McCarthy of Wisconsin. He started making speeches in the early 1950s, accusing everyone from petty bureaucrats in the State Department to General George Marshall, one of the real heroes of the United States Army, of having communist "leanings" or being communist "sympathizers." One journalist said he was a "political speculator who found his gusher." McCarthy, a full-blown alcoholic with massive insecurities, would say and do <u>anything</u> to get attention and approval.

A rumor floated recklessly around campus that our librarian, Mr. Olsen, had "communist ideas". I doubt that any basis existed to foment such a rumor; Mr. Olsen certainly never talked politics with me. He was as patriotic as everyone else was. But the next year he and his family moved to Pennsylvania (which wasn't exactly the Soviet Union.)

Meanwhile, in Washington Senator Joe McCarthy raged in televised hearings which he staged before his Senate committee. Because of a perceived slight by the Army toward a male friend of one of his aides, McCarthy took out after the United States Army, personally attacking individuals instead of merely disagreeing with the wisdom of their opposing ideas.

Television as a medium was not kind to McCarthy. On television he came across as an uncouth bully. I remember seeing McCarthy's downfall on our old black and white TV, when in response to his tirades against an Army officer, and then against an associate of the Army's legal counsel, the distinguished lawyer for the Army, Joseph N. Welch, said:

"Until this moment, Senator, I think I never really gauged your cruelty or your recklessness… let us not assassinate this lad further, Senator. You have done enough. Have you no sense of decency, sir at long last? Have you left no sense of decency?"

People got it. McCarthy's bullying tactics, labeling his enemies Communists without any proof, were soundly repudiated, and McCarthy died of alcoholism, a bitter, exposed loser.

My family voted for Eisenhower, but I believe the following words from his opponent, Adlai Stevenson, speak to us now:

"I want to talk to the great confident majority of Americans, the generous, and the unfrightened, those who are proud of our strength and sure of our goodness, and who want to work with each other in trust."

Of people like McCarthy, he said:

"They call sections of us dupes, and fellow travelers, a man without a purpose and without a mind. But at all times they picture us unworthy, stupid, heartless. They thus betray the hopeful, practical, yet deeply moral America which you and I know."

I believe that the unity which Americans felt during World War II against a common enemy did much to erase or at least to erode some of the prejudices which held society back for generations. We must always beware of politicians who seek to divide us and to appeal to prejudice as a means to win elections. In my view it is a self-serving and downright un-American practice. We have to see every human being as a potential asset who can contribute positively to the continuing American Revolution. Instead of being afraid of ideas, we should debate them openly and with civility.

Finally, God help us if we are ever dumb enough to fall for the condemnation of competent leaders because of their intellect. It should not be a sin to be smart and competent. Let us learn to discern the difference between real ability and manufactured, prepackaged hate speech. We have too good a country populated by too good a citizenry to allow such nonsense.

Mr. Olsen was no more a communist than was my dog Butch.

There is a lot to learn being a paper boy.

Annual Ball

Here it is, the spring of 1956, I'm a freshman at P.A.H.S., and what do they tell me I have to do? Be in the dadgummed Annual Ball. When they first told me I had to be in it, I didn't know what they were talking about. I thought maybe it had something to do with the campus yearbook; you know, the <u>annual</u>? Nope. The dadgummed Annual Ball was a dadgummed <u>dance</u>. They didn't call it a prom. I guess it was a southern thing to call it a ball.

I was not a dancer who had much practice. I mean to be truthful I didn't have <u>any</u> practice whatsoever being Baptist and all. We didn't even <u>kiss</u> a girl standing up for fear people would <u>think</u> we were dancing, it was so frowned down on at our church. I wasn't exactly sure why dancing was such a bad sin but it just <u>was</u>, maybe even higher up on the sin ladder than cussing or smoking cigarettes, and those two particular sins had gotten me on the wrong end of a hickory switch a time or two, let me tell you.

Well it turns out the kind of dancing we would have to show up and learn how to do wasn't technically a sin because it was a <u>waltz</u>. Dancing classes were held at the classroom building across from the cafeteria (the cafeteria that burned down a couple of years later.) Now, waltzing was what we started out learning from this fellow who was a sophomore at the college who said he learned all about dancing in the Air Force. He was stationed at Keesler Field and had a portable phonograph and a whole collection of records. He was an expert waltzer. The waltzes he played on his phonograph for our use were by a famous composer named Strauss, he said.

I was paired up with a nice girl in my class named Meri-Beth who was from Long Beach, Mississippi, where waltzing and other dancing was apparently most definitely <u>not</u> a sin. Meri-Beth was a pretty good waltzer to begin with and she was able to give me some helpful nudges along the lines of proper waltzing and turning and so forth. She was a good sport when I accidently would waltz on her toes or forget to turn when I was supposed to. She was the smartest girl in our class and had blonde hair and a beautiful complexion. She certainly tolerated my lack of waltzing experience in a nice way, for a girl. I felt terrible when I would step on her toes and would try to apologize, but she would just brush it off and say, "never mind," or "that's okay – we are both just learning." She was really nice about it, if you want to know the truth.

The teacher (the college guy from Keesler) had other vinyl records, too. One was "You Send Me" and another was "Rock Around the Clock." I guess they weren't too sinful either, because we learned a little bit about the box step and the jitterbug between waltzes. They were just sidelines to the waltz because they were just dances for general information purposes. But the waltz we had to do because we were going to <u>perform</u> it in front of everybody, so it was the main deal.

The dance teacher guy said waltzing is easy if you just remember to take long steps and always remember that there are <u>three</u> beats to the measure, not four.

Sometimes I forgot to remember but Meri-Beth would help me count. After about three weeks of lessons after school to the same tunes over and over, I was about as ready as I would ever be.

This Annual Ball deal was held in the old Perk Gym which was down the hill from the Administration Building. I wore a rented tuxedo and Meri-Beth had a very pretty white dress. I had a boutonniere and she had a nice corsage. I thought those were interesting words. <u>Cummerbund</u> was another word I had not used really at all until they made me put on that tux.

Meri-Beth was a high school boarding student who lived in Harrison Hall, the girls' dormitory. All the boys in the Annual Ball Court picked up our partners and escorted them walking over across campus to the old gym. They paired us by classes, and Carley Baxter was escorting his fellow high school junior, Eleanor "Cissy" Jordan. I have to tell you, the girls looked really swell in their evening dresses. Cissy and Meri-Beth were friends. All the college and high school boys were called "dukes" and all the girls "duchesses," and let me tell you, they looked the part.

The dukes and duchesses together with the "king" Mac Baker and "queen" Billie Tebbs were the "royal court." And when the time came, let me tell you, the royal court performed the royal waltz. Boy, it was fun, but boy howdy I was glad to get through it without crushing poor Meri-Beth's toes! All the girls said we danced well, and I guess we did because there were no casualties. I remember there were some really young campus kids, David Lipscomb and Hal White decked out in tuxedos as "train bearers" and Mike Clement and a cute little girl named Alice Ann who were the "crown bearers". They kind of stole the show, and all the girls oohed and ahhed over how cute they were.

The old gym was decorated with crepe paper and balloons, and I have to admit it made me feel pretty cool to be sitting up there in a straight chair on the gym floor as part of the "royal court." They had the basketball goal covered with paper colored with carnival type pictures, so the place almost didn't look like the old gym at all. I guess the coach went along with our waltzing on his shiny floor in our regular shoes for that one night because that's what we did.

I can't remember if I walked home or if Mom and Dad picked me up in the old Plymouth, but I reckon dancing turned back into being a sin after the Annual Ball was over because I don't remember doing much dancing or even waltzing at all for at least another year. Meanwhile Elvis had played a show at the Slavonian Lodge in Biloxi and Perry Bond and Elaine Breazeale had gone to it, and my envious concept of sin (because I would have given anything to have been there) had expanded by that time in what our math teacher Mr. Bolthouse would have called <u>geometric</u> proportions.

Icons

Everyone has icons that stand out in life and are memorable. In the advertising world, there were jingles from the 1950s that I still remember floating across the air from neighborhood to neighborhood as I heard the radios of the customers on my newspaper route.

"Brylcream, a little dab'll do ya, Brylcream, you'll look so debonair.

Brylcream, the gals will pursue ya, Simply rub a little in your hair."

I can honestly say that I never recall using Brylcream, and I didn't "get Wildroot Cream Oil, Charlie," either, but I can still hear those jingles assailing my ears as I rode my trusty Western Flyer bicycle around Perkinston. Advertising created plenty of iconic symbols for us.

There were also plenty of living, breathing icons whom I also would encounter along my paper route. In the faculty hall, Colonel Bob Rivers, the college registrar and dean of instruction, was definitely an icon. He always had some words of wisdom for me. I remember pedaling up and handing him his paper one warm, spring afternoon and his musing, "My boy, some people use the word 'politician' as though it is a curse word; but you must <u>never</u> do that... a 'politician,' my boy, is one who is <u>schooled in the science of government</u>." I listened and still remember what Colonel Bob said, and I have to admit I have had lapses at times from adhering to his admonition, but I have also had numerous occasions to seek some solace in his idealism, particularly when confronted (and I have been) with politicians behaving badly. His words are right up there with Dr. Martin Luther King's "Despair is not an option," because coming from an icon like Colonel Bob, they impressed me.

A more genial icon for me was the long time guidance director and Dean, C. G. Odom. He was one of the finest guys ever in my book. Modest, soft-spoken, a tough ex-military man, he was full of kindness and genuine concern for young people and an inspiration to me and to many hundreds of students who came in contact with him. He paid his paper bill faithfully and always had a word of encouragement.

People of the stature of our high school principal, J. V. Wentzell, Coach J. V. Shiel, Professor Eugene Clement and our band director, Professor Sam Jones, were rare individuals, unforgettable characters who imparted character to those students privileged to know them.

Prof. Jones would get Prof. Clement to help him arrange the music for the band, and I remember his recounting how until they recruited Frances Hemeter to help choreograph the Perkettes in their dance routines, the two of them would try to invent moves for that delightful dance team.

Professor Jones, usually serious in his demeanor, could make anybody laugh as he demonstrated how he and Professor "Clem" would try a move and then say to each other, "Do you think that will look right?" Both of them were terrific and inspiring music educators, but to hear Professor Jones tell it, as choreographers, they were lousy.

It was fun knowing the characters on my paper route, pedaling my Western Flyer, hair blowing in the breeze, not caring a flip about debonair.

A Night at the Opera

You will not believe how being a Perk paperboy got me all the way to New Orleans to see my first and only opera. I have mentioned that the English teacher Helen Murphy was one of my customers. She had three pretty daughters so I delivered her paper <u>right on time</u>.

Well, she was going to take two of her daughters Helen and Kathleen along with one of their friends Carol Downes (who lived in Pass Christian, Mississippi) to New Orleans to the <u>opera</u>. It was <u>Carmen</u>, by composer Georges Bizet. Would I care to accompany them? You bet!

Traveling in Mrs. Murphy's 1952 Ford, we first went from Perkinston to Pass Christian to pick up Miss Downes, then over the Bay St. Louis Bridge, westward on Highway 90, over the Rigolets Bridge across Lake Ponchatrain, then to Chef Menteur Highway into New Orleans to the opera; a <u>looong</u> trip in the 1950s!

I'm wearing a suit and a bow tie and feeling very worldly and sophisticated, eyeballing everything in the opera house, then hearing the orchestra tune up and then the famous prelude. I remember they called the intermission the <u>interlude</u>, and there was a bar to get cokes and seven-ups and probably stronger fare for the adults.

Now <u>Carmen</u> is one of the three or four best loved operas of all time. Bizet poured every ounce of his genius into it, and when it opened in 1875 in Paris and was not a commercial success, he died at age 37 of a heart attack. It is all in French, which, thanks to Miss Susie Cooley, my modern language teacher back at PAHS, I was learning. I couldn't understand the words, but they sounded <u>really</u>

<u>French</u>, but it was all right because right there in the program was an English translation, whew!

Carmen is a bad, fine-looking Gypsy girl who works in a cigarette factory in Seville, Spain, circa 1830. She has an attitude and a passionate flair, and, oh yes, a temper.

Don Jose, (pronounced "Joe-Zay") an inexperienced corporal in the army, falls for her fully and fatefully. His obsession with this hussy Carmen leads him to reject his very nice girlfriend, Micaela, disobey his superior officer and turn to a life of crime. His obsession turns into madness when (you could have guessed) Carmen throws him over for a romantic bullfighter, a toreador named Escamillo. Of course Don Jose then up and kills Carmen. He should have left her alone in the first place. But I'm getting ahead of myself.

The first time they meet, Carmen is taunted by Jose's fellow soldiers, all of them asking when she will love them, who will she choose, etc., and in reply she throws a flower in front of Jose. <u>Baaad vibes</u>.

She fights with another girl in the factory and slashes the girl's face with a knife. Jose is ordered to arrest her and escort her to jail. She seduces him with a song and convinces him to let her escape, for which Jose himself is arrested. (Told you he should have left her alone.)

Jose's commanding officer, Zuniga, even makes a pass at Carmen, but since Jose is about to be let out of jail, she only has eyes for Jose. Then the toreador Escamillo comes along, and – what else?-- Carmen even goes for him!

Jose zoots in fresh from the hoosegow, and Carmen dances for him; then when the C.O., Zuniga, surprises them, Jose draws his sword on him. The Gypsies take the C.O. away, Jose is forced to flee with Carmen, and you will not believe what happens next.

You will recall Jose is head over his soldier's boots in love with Carmen and has committed the crime of letting her escape from his custody and even mutinied against his own commanding officer when they go off into the mountains to join her smuggler pals. Carmen soon tires of poor old Jose who is too weak for her tastes and instead big-loves her beautiful bullfighter (Think Toreador song.)

Carmen's girlfriends read the cards and see good stuff for themselves, but death for Carmen.

Micaela (Jose's girlfriend) arrives looking for Jose but hides when she hears a gunshot.

Escamillo da bullfighter arrives and tells Jose that he is in love with a gypsy girl who has fallen for a soldier, (not realizing the soldier is Jose – whoops! <u>Embarrassing</u>!)

Jose and Escamillo's fight is narrowly averted by the smugglers, and Micaela comes to tell Jose he has to go see his mother who is dying, like, <u>right now</u>. As he is leaving, Escamillo da bullfighter is singing in the distance, and Carmen skips off to follow him.

We are outside the arena, where Escamillo and Carmen arrive with the crowd cheering them. Escamillo tells Carmen he never loved anybody as much as he loves her. Carmen's girlfriend warns her that Jose is in the crowd and that he intends to kill her, but Carmen says not to worry, she'll talk to him. Before she goes into the arena, Jose appears, in despair, demanding that she love him. Of course she tells him she no longer cares for him and throws his ring back in his face, so he just ups and stabs her in the heart – <u>sayonara to the senorita</u>! She dies at the moment Escamillo triumphs in the arena. As the spectators exit, Jose, completely broken, confesses that he killed her. The End. <u>Loser</u>!

All right, enough about this opera, but I have to admit it made an impression on me. I can't believe my parents let me go to it, that I even wanted to go to it, and that I actually found it enjoyable. How could love and death with a beautiful gypsy girl, a forlorn soldier, and a romantic bullfighter possibly be interesting?

Bam! We are back in Mrs. Murphy's Ford, treking east to Mississippi via Pass Christian, getting home Lord knows how late.

These torrid toreador tales tempted teenage testosterone, but here was one plumb tuckered paperboy plenty pleased to park pronto back in Perk!

Life Is But A Dream

The other day I was thinking about how the college campus at Perk looked when we moved there in 1946. Dad took the job as dean of men and I remember as an eager four-year-old waiting for the movers to come and get our meager furniture from the house we had occupied in Johnston Station, Mississippi, which is just south of McComb. Dad had been the school superintendent there. The reason our furniture was meager is that the first big old ramshackled frame house we lived in had a wood stove, and one day while mom was cooking cornbread, a fire ignited in the stovepipe and the house burned to the ground. What a trauma!

Dad moved us into a smaller house and we took along the few pieces of furniture that they were able to save before the house completely burned. I remember that he finished the school year and would go to work every day wearing khakis instead of a suit because all of our clothes burned up in the fire. As if it were an indelible photograph, I remember everyone in the little village of Johnston Station lining the gravel road in front of the house as it was burning down.

Moving to the Perk campus was like moving to another world. The buildings were all built in classic architectural style, and we moved into a nice apartment on the first floor of Varsity Hall which is now called Jackson Hall. The president of the college was A. L. May, a kind and distinguished man whose pet phrase for praising anyone– students, faculty, maintenance crew, or wide-eyed little boys, was "Mighty fine!"

Dad had to contend with the influx of veterans who came to the college to be educated after World War II, thanks to the "G.I.

Bill," which paid for their education. Many were seasoned veterans who had seen combat and served their country in Europe, the South Pacific, and all of the other corners of the World War, so Dad balanced firm discipline with a sensible "rule of reason," realizing that these young men were due a little latitude, given their recent service. One night, for example Dad and I were sitting by Varsity Hall on one of those old benches which had concrete at each end and two by four seats and backs. It was at the moment when dusk passes into night time, and I said to Dad, "Here comes old Cowboy and Picket and the other boys. Aren't you going to say hello to them?" In a low voice my Dad said, "No son, not tonight." I was later told by a member of that cohort that they had been up to the Toot 'N Tell It for a couple of beers. If Dad had "caught" them with alcohol breath on them, he would have been bound to report their conduct, and any drinking was a "shipping" offense. In other words, they could have been expelled from school, but for the fact that Dad applied his "rule of reason" and managed to ignore any transgression in these good men fresh home from the late war. They respected Dad for it and gave him the nickname of "Old Square Deal."

The college swimming pool had not been built back in those days so there was a very long sidewalk that ran from the old library (later called Bennett Hall) all the way down the hill. Those benches with concrete ends and two-by-four slats placed under shady trees made for a great visiting area for the campus moms while they watched all of us playing on the wide expanses of lawn.

Between Jackson Hall and The Freshman Dorm (now called Huff Hall) there was a small, old concrete pool that my Dad plastered up and fixed to be a little swimming pool where most of us kids learned how to swim. Just by it was a large Mimosa Tree that we would climb and whose exotic gossamer blossoms would float to the ground when the breezes would catch them.

I remember one sweet summer afternoon when all of us were out by the little swimming pool and Mr. and Mrs. J. V. Gammage came walking by, and Mr. Gammage was carrying a beautiful vase that had been in their family forever, and it was full of white Gladiolas, and as he was walking along you could hear the water sloshing in the vase. He said he had drunk so much of Mrs. Gammage's iced tea at lunch, it was sloshing around inside him, and all of us laughed and laughed.

Those lazy bygone days remind me of Poe's lines:

> "Take this kiss upon the brow!
> And, parting from you now,
> This much let me avow–
> You are not wrong, who deem
> That my days have been a dream;
> Yet if hope has flown away
> In a night, or in a day,
> In a vision, or in none
> Is it therefore the less <u>gone</u>?
> All that we see or seem
> Is but a dream within a dream."

Growing up in Perk was fun. Sometime, when you want to hear of sentimental journeys and dreams, I'll tell you about it.

Small Miracles

I think I was in the fifth or sixth grade when we got our first television set, a Zenith model purchased from Hall's in Wiggins. I remember the first night we watched it in the living room, and Dad and I saw a prize fight. It was a miracle seeing those two fighters slugging it out in glorious black and white on the small screen.

One of my favorite shows was Texaco Star Theater with Milton Berle. Uncle Milty or "Mr. Television," as he liked to be called, cracked jokes, threw pies, sang off-key, and even dressed up in women's clothes; anything to get a laugh. He would caper around doing slapstick comedy with guests like Martha Raye, or Jack Benny, or even Elvis.

As I have said, we citizens of Perkinston were easily amused. As a kid, I remember Buffalo Bob and all his gang on The Howdy Doody Show and on Saturday morning seeing Sky King, and later Hopalong Cassidy. Cowboys were cool.

I remember Elvis' appearance on The Ed Sullivan Show when they made a big deal of the fact that the cameras were forbidden from showing Elvis' body from the waist down, presumably because his gyrations would corrupt American youth everywhere. I remember watching the Andrea Doria ocean liner sink, live, on TV, and watching Queen Elizabeth's coronation in Westminister Abbey. All these were historic moments, but one of the most memorable for me occurred during the first game of the 1954 World Series between the favored Cleveland Indians and the beleaguered New York Giants. It was the day Willie Mays' made the catch, and I saw the whole thing on our black and white TV on our back porch.

The Indians had dominated the American League that year, winning 111 games to clench the pennant. The scene at the Polo Grounds was tense because the score was tied 2-2 in the eighth with Cleveland at bat.

The Giants' pitcher Sal Maglie walked Larry Doby, and Cleveland's Al Rosen got a little base hit to put two men on base with nobody out. The next Indian up was Vic Wertz, a left handed batter who was already three for three against Maglie. I was pulling for the underdog Giants.

The Giants manager Leo Durocher took Sal Maglie off the mound and sent in Don Liddle, a left handed relief pitcher. On the first pitch Vic Wertz hit the ball so hard that my heart sank – I, along with all who watched, just knew Wertz had hit a homer. It would've put the Indians ahead three runs. But we underestimated Willie Mays.

Mays, at the crack of Wertz's bat, started running from his position in left center field, dead away from the trajectory of the hammered ball. It seemed impossible that he could catch it unless he had eyes in the back of his head or unless his instinctive judgment and skill were a miraculous gift.

We watched him run with our jaws dropped, hoping against hope...

Later, Mays said:

"I saw it clearly. As soon as I picked it out of the sky, I knew I had to get toward center field. I turned and ran out full speed toward center with my back to the plate. But even as I was running, I realized I had to be in stride if I was going to catch it, so about 450 feet away from the plate I looked up over my left shoulder and could see the ball. I timed it perfectly and it dropped into my glove maybe 10 or 15 feet from the bleacher wall. At that same moment I wheeled and threw in one motion and fell to the ground. I must have looked like a corkscrew. I could feel my hat flying off, but I saw the ball heading straight to Davey Williams on second. Davey grabbed the relay and threw home, Doby had tagged up at second after the catch. That held Doby on third...while Rosen had to get back to first very quickly."

The catch broke the mighty Indians; the Giants went on to win that day and swept the series 4-0.

I remember a similar catch made by George Jordan one afternoon on the Perk Elementary School campus during a game when he wheeled and threw the ball from center field all the way across home plate, a perfect strike, enabling the catcher to tag the base runner and win the game for our team. In Perk we had our own miracles so TV baseball was just good entertainment.

Friends and Neighbors

By this time you understand that it was my privilege as the paperboy of Perk to grow up knowing some wonderful people. Our little town had its share of characters, but when I used to hear that old 40s song "I love those dear hearts and gentle people, who live and love in my home town," I knew in <u>my</u> heart the lyrics were referring to Perkinston, Mississippi.

One memorable and wonderful couple on my paper route were our next to next door neighbors, Mr. and Mrs. Jowann Dedeaux, whom I referred to as Mr. Joe and Mrs. Ruby. To say they were stalwart citizens is an understatement. Each of them had that blossom of sincere Christian spirit about them that needed no words to convey their strength of character and goodness.

Mr. Joe grew up in Pearl River County and went off to fight in World War I. When he arrived in France, he had a distinct advantage over his fellow soldiers because in the home where he grew up, P'ere and M'ere Dedeaux and all of their clan spoke French so he could converse with the people he had to come to liberate and serve as interpreter for his fellow soldiers.

He returned home to become an R.F.D. ("Rural Free Delivery") mail carrier and had the longest mail route in the United States.

He met his bride to be, Miss Ruby Randall, a Biloxi girl who had finished Mississippi Southern, class of 1916, and come to educate the youth of the Silver Run community in Stone County. Mrs. Ruby was such a sweet person that I can readily understand how Mr. Joe could fall for her. He was reported to say (as her mail carrier) that if a day came when she didn't get a letter, he would just write her one himself.

Mr. Joe and Mrs. Ruby lived two houses south of us, and they were more than just paper route customers because I would see them every time we went to the Perkinston Baptist Church. They both were faithful leaders in the church and just lived their faith instead of talking about it.

Mr. Joe used to grow a patch of giant bamboo cane which made great fishing poles. I always remember that when Mrs. Ruby paid her paper bill, she would invite me to have some cookies or a piece of cake. In my book, they were both tops. It is no wonder their son, Randall Dedeaux, who became a consultant forester was such a good guy. He and his wife, Zettie Bond Dedeaux (daughter of Mr. and Mrs. Palmus Bond) were leading citizens in Perkinston, and their sons John Randall and Edwin turned out to be good guys, too.

In our little community, knowing wholesome, stable, secure adults gave us the freedom to be children.

To know such people as Mr. Joe and Mrs. Ruby was what it was like to be a child growing up in Perkinston. In the words of the writer Francis Thompson, "It is to be something very different from the man of today. It is to have a spirit yet streaming from the waters of baptism; it is to believe in love, to believe in loveliness, to believe in belief; it is to be so little that the elves can reach to whisper in your ear; it is to turn pumpkins into coaches, and mice into horses, lowness into loftiness, and nothing into everything, for every child has its fairy godmother in its own soul; it is to live in a nutshell and to count yourself the king of infinite space; it is

> To see a world in a grain of sand,
> And a heaven in a wild flower,
> Hold infinity in the palm of your hand,
> And eternity in an hour;

It is to know not as yet that you are under sentence of life..." In short, it was like a splash in Red Creek on the first day of Summer! Sometime I'll tell you about some of the other dear hearts and gentle people whom I knew on my paper route.

Foxhunting Memories

Brethren and sisters, if you have never leaned back and listened to a foxhunt on a cool, quiet South Mississippi moonlit night, you have missed some of the sweetest music this side of Beulah. When I was growing up, my Dad always kept several top notch hounds; none of them were registered, but each of them had good mouths, plenty of stamina and grit, and we knew their mixed ancestry was from stock that had been naturally born to give Monsieur Reynard all the chase he ever wanted to handle.

The leader of the pack was old Boston; he was a chopmouthed part Walker, July and Birdsong. We had a strike dog named Bell, a part Bluetick bitch that must have graduated from a foxhunting school in her youth because, try as he might, the wily Mr. Bushytail could never outsmart her like he did some of the other dogs. On a still night, Bell's horn mouth could make the hair stand up on the back of your neck. Walleye, Black Gal, and a couple of hound comrades-in-arms belonging to a neighbor and bosom foxhunting buddy rounded out the pack. Not a one of those dogs would run anything but a fox; none of them would bark on a covered trail, and none of them would quit before the race was over.

Before you feel too sorry for the poor old fox set against these formidable odds, you must know and understand that the woods were full of them, mostly grays but a good many reds, and every one more than adept at proving his ancestral trait of using every possible artifice to elude his pursuers. A fox, in addition to being naturally born fast, has an uncanny sense of direction and an unbelievable ability to outwit most dogs. I remember the men remarking as there would come a lull in the race and then the dogs would start up again that "He switched foxes on them." That meant that the pursued fox was running a sort of relay with his mate, with Mr. and Mrs. Reynard crossing each other's paths in an effort to throw the dogs off the track. Doubling back on the same trail was kid stuff to these educated South Mississippi foxes, and since many races were ended without killing the fox by the hunters voluntarily catching the dogs, most of them held post graduate degrees in elusiveness conferred by Boston and Bell.

Before you imagine that we dressed up in red riding breeches and funny hats to go on a foxhunt, let me tell you the way it was. We didn't use horses at all; we would just load up the dogs in the Jeep and take them out to the place they usually struck a trail. With flashlights, or by moonlight, the hunters would search in the sandy ditches bordering the graveled country roads for a fresh fox track, and when they found one they would bring out Bell. Bell was the "strike" dog. If she didn't strike his trail right away, we would pick up and find another place. Usually you would hear her horn mouth telling us to turn the other dogs loose to join her and telling the fox that they had some urgent business to conclude.

A stealthy fox will usually run in an area not much greater than that within hearing distance, and much of the enjoyment of the hunt is in knowing by the sound of their voices what dogs are doing the chasing.

A good foxhunter can tell where his dogs are, and which one is in the lead, and how close they are to the fox. Just by listening, he is getting a play-by-play description from his dogs.

Sometimes in winter we would build a fire and sit around it and listen to them run. One race I remember where Bell really proved her mettle occurred in Harrison County woods at a place where three dirt-surface logroads, each about four or five miles long, conjoined to make a triangle. The surface of the logroads was hard and smooth. It was a bright moonlit night, and when the fox and the dogs would make a close pass, you could actually see them running like phantoms, stealing across the floor of the pine woods. The cutting edge of pine straw is hard on a dog's feet, and I guess the fox had the same problem because that night he would run out of hearing, come back, and then trace the triangle of the logroads. The dogs were laying in there following him out of hearing, back in again, and then around the triangle. Then an amazing thing happened: the fox came by <u>within sight of us</u> and ran his course as if he were going to run the logroad triangle again; only <u>this time</u> he <u>didn't</u> run the logroad– instead, he jumped as far as he could, just like lightning, from the trail he had been following out into the brush and loped off in a different direction into the woods. The first time the fox pulled this trick the dogs ran the triangle and the fox gained some valuable time. The same ploy outsmarted all of the dogs the second time, for they kept laying on the trail he had left on the logroad; all of them, that is, <u>except Bell</u>. When she hung back, circled through the brush and sounded her horn, I knew she was a real foxhound; but when the other dogs joined her, I was convinced she was a legend. Well, sir, that was one fox that wound up in a gopher hole that night. Instead of cutting a longleaf sapling, peeing on it, and running it down the hole to flush out the fox, we left that one to discuss his narrow escape with Mr. Land Tortoise, to whom he was paying the unexpected visit, and called in the dogs.

> Remembering the hunt, it had been like the one Shakespeare once described:
>
> "...Never did I hear
> Such gallant chiding, for besides the groves,
> The skies, the fountains, every region near
> Seemed all one mutual cry. I never heard
> So musical a discord, such sweet thunder."

That night (and on many other ones, too) Bell earned her place in the hall of fame of those worthy to hold the title conferred by the Bard of Avon upon such hounds, when he said:

"My hounds are bred out of the Spartan kind,
So flewed, so sanded; and their heads are hung
With ears that sweep away the morning dew...
Fast in pursuit, and matched in mouth like bells,
Each under each.
...A cry more tunable

Was never holloed to, nor cheered with horn."

    There will never be another Bell. Half the foxes in South Mississippi are resting easier now that she is gone, and the other half are still telling tales about her.

Perk Baptist Church

As the poet said, "How dear to this heart are the scenes of my childhood, when fond recollection presents them to view!" One of my fondest recollections is of the Perkinston Baptist Church in which I was baptized and raised.

The church I remember was in a quaint old white clapboard building across from the Perkinston Elementary School. I loved it because it was small and familiar and had about it a friendly and reverent atmosphere. When I walked in, I knew everybody instantly and all of us came together to worship. I remember seeing the numbers mounted on the little black felt board that hung on the wall to the left of the baptistry every Sunday. That told us how many members we had, how many were in attendance last Sunday, how many were in Sunday School, and what hymns we would be singing during the service. Thinking back on it, the number of church members was about the same as the number of customers on my paper route. While I delivered papers to plenty of folks who were not members of our church, most of my fellow parishioners were also my paper route customers. On Sundays (usually) "I was glad when they said unto me, 'Let us go into the house of the Lord'" because there I was sure to find friendly faces.

In school chapel we used to sing about "The Little Brown Church in the Vale", and while our building was white, and not brown, and it was on the hill, not in the vale, the words of that old song could have otherwise described our wonderful little church:

"There's a church in the valley by the wildwood,
No lovelier spot in the dale;
No place is so dear to my childhood
As the little brown church in the vale..."

***

"How sweet on a clear Sabbath morning,
To list to the clear ringing bell;
Its tones so sweetly are calling,
Oh come to the church in the vale."

I remember Sundays as a time of hustling to put on our best clothes (I had a pair of tan shoes with tan shoelaces from Yeager's Drygoods that I loved to wear) and loading up in the car and trying to make it to Sunday School on time. Usually we were successful, generally by the skin of our teeth, in the nick of time.

We had a number of ministers, and three I remember were Dr. Robert Darby, Reverend Aaron Foy, and Dr. Don Stewart. They were all outstanding, great people, and we were so lucky to have them. One day on my paper route, I saw Dr. Don Stewart (who went on to become president of William Carey College) emerge from his home, the "pastorium," with a very big lipstick smudge, smack on his mouth. His lovely wife Mona had obviously kissed him goodbye as he strode purposefully out to go about visiting the sick, ministering to the elderly and inspiring the youth and adult population of our community. He was such a fine man, and I remember feeling good that with all of his learning, and all his devotion to duty, and all the sacrifices I knew he made for our community, that he was also wonderfully human.

If the sun came up on Sunday morning, you could count on Albert Earl McDonald being in the church vestibule to hand you your church bulletin, which contained the order of service and announcements and some inspiring words of the Southern Baptist variety. Likewise, on the left row of pews, second pew, you would see Joe and Ruby Dedeaux and their son Randall. His wife Zettie

Dedeaux would be playing the piano or organ. Gregory Davis was there and Mr. and Mrs. Willie Rogers and so many others.

We would sing "Stand up, Stand up for Jesus," and "On Jordan's Stormy Banks I Stand," and "The Old Rugged Cross." Once during Sunday school, Mrs. Davis was passing out Crayola Crayons, asking each child what color he or she wanted. When she asked my little brother David who was about four years old at the time, "What'll you have?," he responded "Pabst Blue Ribbon!" Everybody laughed. While my own keen sense of guilt was doubtless to some extent honed in that church, I do not actually recall too much fire and brimstone being thrown at us; our pastors were real scholars and lived their faith so they just mostly sought to educate and inspire us. Our church was a place of love, not condemnation.

The people whom I was lucky enough to know in Perkinston left an indelible impression on me. When we sang "What a friend we have in Jesus," we had good examples of friendship standing all around us.

At the Movies

The other day I watched an old movie on television that I know my parents didn't let me see back in 1956 at the Straub Theatre on Pine Street. It was "Invasion of the Body Snatchers," and while it is a good scary movie, it is pretty tame compared to today's cinema fare.

The Straub Theatre and its sister theatre, the Glo Drive-In, were the source of much of our first teenage movie adventures during the 1950s. Many of us had our first dates there, so the plots of the movies may be kind of incidental. What I do remember is that it was a special event to get to go to the "picture show"! Popcorn, a coke, and, whether you had a date or not, rest assured that you could settle back in your seat for some movie magic!

I remember seeing lots of "shoot-em-ups," as we called the cowboy movies, and plenty of Hollywood musicals and comedies. To this day I laugh when I think about Danny Kaye in "The Court Jester" in comic desperation, as a sort of clownish Robin Hood impersonating the Court Jester, on a mission to, well, restore the rightful heir to the English throne, trying to remember which glass contained the poison the bad guys were trying to trick him into drinking. He closed his eyes and recited the rhyme, "The Pellet with the poison's in the vessel with the pestle. The chalice from the palace holds the brew that is true." It's a great, wholesome comedy from 1956. There were the Abbott and Costello movies which were also hilarious, and Martin and Lewis were funny and silly.

In 1957 I got my driver's license and took a date to "An Affair to Remember" with Cary Grant and Deborah Kerr. It was way over my head, and that's about all I remember about it. On the other hand, I always have remembered the plot of "The Bridge on the River Kwai," also from 1957, and have enjoyed seeing it many times since that premiere occasion at the Straub. There were plenty of war movies, some starring Audie Murphy who was a real soldier and one of the most decorated men in World War II. He was a soft spoken guy, and when he acted, you could believe he was a real war hero.

There were lots of Biblical movies in the 1950s from "The Robe," with a young guy named Richard Burton and an equally young Jean Simmons, "Sampson and Delilah" with Victor Mature, and several with a young Charlton Heston playing everyone from Moses to Ben-Hur.

Science Fiction was also big in the 50s. "The Day the Earth Stood Still," "When Worlds Collide," and other apocalyptic shows took our minds off the real worries we had about the atomic bomb and the arms race with Russia.

Drive-in movies declined when every household got a television. It is kind of sad because the drive-in experience was very social. You would pull your vehicle up to the speaker stand, roll down the windows, hook the speaker to the car window, and settle in for family entertainment. People at the Glo Drive In would circulate as they went to the refreshment stand, speaking to their neighbors; it was all pretty public in nature, <u>sans</u> air conditioning, with the movie being played out on a gigantic screen. I know drive-ins were noted as places for romantic encounters, but looking back on it, the whole community was sitting in the parking lot with you in their respective cars. If it takes a village to raise a teenager, they supplied the village! I can still see Jesse Thomas in his cool part-time job carrying the heavy boxes across that parking lot with the reels of film to be shown at the Glo Drive-In.

I like movies with happy endings.

Maybe life is like a movie in some respects. One poet aptly expressed it:

> "I see not a step before me as I tread on another year;
> But I've left the past in God's keeping,
> The future His mercy clear;
> And what looks dark in the distance,
> May brighten as I draw near."

Growing up in Perkinston meant living life one day at a time. God as we knew him did not send down day-old bread; our days were fresh baked, full of adventure and mystery, and lots of fun!

A Lodge of Masons

Among my fond childhood memories are the times spent in the village of Perkinston when Dad would take us to the family functions held at the J.L. Power Lodge. The old lodge hall was a two story white frame building located north of the railroad track next door to Randall Dedeaux's home (and office), just a couple of blocks east of Dees Store. The historic building housed J.L. Power Lodge, Number 416, which was named after the distinguished Mississippian, John Logan Power who was the Confederate Grave Registration officer who served for 32 years as the First Grand Secretary of the Grand Lodge of Mississippi and who was an honorary past Grand Master of that statewide organization.

The old lodge hall was built entirely of lumber, and its interior showed the finely grained heart yellow pine and beaded ceilings that graced buildings and homes in the 19th century.

My Dad served as master of the lodge in 1949, and he took his membership in the masonic order very seriously. Many of the members were leading citizens and friends who were also good customers on my paper route. My Mom patiently fixed coffee and entertained wives of initiates when they would come up to the homestead for my Dad to "lecture" the novices in their degrees. Mom was in the Eastern Star so she put up with Dad going out to the back forty with the new members to impart all the "secrets" to them. One of my most treasured possessions is my Dad's <u>Blue Lodge Text Book</u>, and inscribed on the inside cover he wrote his name with the date "February 21, 1947 – W.D. Smith was Secretary." Mr. Smith taught woodworking and other vocational studies at Perkinston Jr. College and was a great friend when my Dad was Dean of Men at the College.

Dad would take us to fish fries, officer installation nights and other open social functions at the lodge, and I recall his telling me that the building was at one time used as a school building and that he actually taught school there as a young man. My Dad was a natural teacher and made education his career, and it is easy for me to see how his curiosity and delight in knowledge led him to become a Mason as soon as he was old enough to join the lodge. His grandfather Anderson Harper Blackwell used to ride his mule from the Success Community in Harrison County down to the Polar Star lodge in Handsboro where my uncle Homer Blackwell was later a member so it was natural that Dad was also attracted to the masonic fellowship.

Since some of the fraternal masonic rituals are secret, many misconceptions and lots of ignorance have arisen among some people about freemasonry. Recently many books and movies have popularized the mysterious and secret side of the ancient and honorable institution, but the real heart and soul of the Order is in the principles recognizing the existence of God, the immortality of the soul, and love for mankind. These principles are the "secret" key to why the fellowship has survived for so many centuries. So to me the organization based on these principles is not at all secret. Masonry is not, however, a religion or a substitute for church.

These foundational principles, however, can be seen through the lives of notable people who have been members of this fraternity such as George Washington, Benjamin Franklin, and countless other world leaders, writers, scientists, artists, teachers, astronauts and tradesmen on every continent.

One of the dividends of my life was that my Dad conferred all three of my lodge degrees, and the friendships he had and the principles he lived from the masonic tradition still benefit and enrich my life.

J.L. Power Lodge is still going strong in Perkinston and continues to be an influence for good in the community. I am honored to be a member of such a vibrant lodge. It is an institution like the lodge at

Kilwinning, Scotland, where the poet Robert Burns was a member. To the "Men and Brethern" there he wrote:

> "Within this dear mansion may wayward contention or withered envy ne'er enter! May secrecy round be the mystical bound and brotherly love be the center!"

Masons do not really recruit new members. They just do good things in their community, enjoy the fellowship in the lodge, and try to be good citizens. So any man who is interested in becoming a Mason should just ask a lodge member about joining this worthy fellowship. It meant a lot to my Dad, and it still means a lot to me.

Perk beat Pearl River!

Before I ever dreamed of becoming the Perk Paperboy, I was one of the "campus kids" at the college. My Dad moved us to Perkinston in 1946, where he served post-war Perkinston Junior College as dean of men.

From my standpoint, being a campus kid had immense advantages. We lived in an apartment in Varsity Hall (now called Jackson Hall). My Dad would let me go with him when he went to check on the boys. He made the rounds through our dorm and made certain that everyone was present and accounted for. When I roomed in Jackson Hall later as a Perk student, we _still_ had to sign in and out.

My Mom would visit with the other campus wives. In good weather they would sit on the benches, usually the ones at the top of the hill in front of the Science Building which also housed the High School and Library.

In the Fall they took me to the football games which were played on the old athletic field across the railroad tracks at the bottom of the hill. There was always an air of anticipation on a crisp autumn day, and one game is to this day one of my favorite memories. I was six years old; the year was 1948.

Perk had a great team that year. I didn't realize it at the time, but the Bulldogs had won all seven of their games, going into the November 6 game against Pearl River Junior College. I just remember the crisp afternoon in the bleachers on the west side of the field. (A.L. May Memorial Stadium had not yet been built).

Dad bought Mom a yellow mum corsage with a blue "PJC" in the middle of the flower. I guess they had a sitter to stay with my five-month old brother during the game. All of us wanted to cheer for the Bulldogs, and we were fortunate to have seats in the bleachers because many spectators had to stand throughout the game.

Leading the Bulldogs was quarterback Bobby Holmes, a naturally gifted athlete who could run and pass exceptionally well. He hit a young player, an end from Perkinston named Ed Evans with a pass that set up the first score by the Bulldogs. Then the tide turned in favor of Coach Dobie Holden's Wildcats. By the fourth quarter they had scored nineteen points to put the Bulldogs down 19-7.

In the fourth quarter, Bobby Holmes passed the ball to wingback Davis Melton, a pass which spotted the ball on the Wildcats' three yard line. Nimrod Ellis scored for the Bulldogs, and with the extra point, the score was 19-14, in favor of Pearl River. Hopes were high.

On the next drive the Bulldogs were stopped by the Pearl River defense on the <u>one</u> yard line! We were getting pretty worried.

The Bulldogs were in a tight spot, and our crowd in the bleachers was very subdued. Victory had seemed so close...then one of the band members, a long, lanky trombone player named Bobby Lefeve (later he became an outstanding dentist in Gulfport) came down out of the stands and took his place by the Perk cheerleaders. Grabbing a megaphone, Bobby, whom everybody called "Old Crow," started a spontaneous cheer that was so infectious it got everyone in the crowd yelling for the Bulldogs. It was incredible, electric, and very exciting!

William Ashton "Picket" Randall who played almost every minute of the game says that quarterback Bobby Holmes, hearing the overwhelming loud ruckus Old Crow was leading and that the fans were kicking up there in the grandstands, and knowing that the game probably turned on the next play, looked to the sidelines and coach "Red" Campbell for the crucial instruction – "what do we do?" It was fourth down. Campbell was so flummoxed upon meeting Holmes's plaintive gaze that he only managed cluelessly to roll his eyes, head, and elevated nose as though he were delivering the whole outcome of the game up to the remote and inscrutable gods of football. Holmes, realizing then that he had to take charge, called a little play where, upon receiving the ball from center, he executed a turn as if he were going to run the ball himself but instead bootlegged it to Davis Melton, who ran for the winning touchdown.

Dr. Charles Sullivan in his wonderful book <u>Mississippi Gulf Coast Community College: A History,</u> says,

"In the words of the <u>Daily Herald</u> reporter covering the game, 'Holmes lost a yard, then dashed to the 11. He lost another yard and on the fourth down gave a hand-off to Melton who propelled around right end for the touchdown that put the Bulldogs ahead.' The Bulldogs won the razor edged thriller 20-19."

I remember my Dad being happy and kissing my Mom on the way home. I think she was pretty happy, too.

Sometime when you have a minute, I'll tell you about the time I dove into the college pond that used to be located down by the President's home (now the Alumni House), and about how my Dad would take me by the old power house to see the interesting machinery. The power house had an old coal fired steam engine that generated the electricity for the college until the community of Perkinston became connected to the Mississippi Power Company's electric distribution system. It was a neat place to visit.

I'm Still Pedaling

After reading these old stories, I hope you have a sense of what it was like for a kid to grow up in Perkinston, Mississippi, in the 1950s. Years later someone from another state remarked that I was from one of the poorest counties in the poorest State in the United States. I was taken aback by that statement because even though I knew we weren't rich while I was spending my childhood growing up in Perkinston, I never once felt impoverished.

Maybe the reason was initially because our family lived in an apartment in a two-storey brick dormitory amidst the stately architecture on the campus of Perkinston Junior College. We had moved there in 1946, several months after our home in Johnston Station, Mississippi, was completely destroyed by fire. As a four year old, I thought since we lived in a big brick "house" we must be doing all right.

Since then I have realized that the neighbors and friends my family knew in Perkinston, and in Stone County, Mississippi, made us welcome and were generally supportive and encouraging, so our spirits were not impoverished. As we thought in our hearts that we were nurtured and enriched by the experience of community, so we were indeed.

Everything was not rosy – the fear of polio, the sadness of the Korean War (in which one of my cousins was terribly wounded), the cancerous taint of racial prejudice and segregation, the repressive fears encouraged by McCarthyism, and the ignorance and lack of education that contribute to so much poverty even today – none of these clouds were pleasant, and none of them evoke good memories.

But the simplicity of our family life, the fun of inexpensive togetherness, being at once close to the country life and close to a center of education (the junior college at Perkinston), and having reliable institutions around which to center our lives – the church, the school, scouting, the lodge hall (just to mention a few) more than compensated for the negative forces, particularly when seen through the eyes of a child.

Our town was by no means perfect, and looking back I can see that there were opportunities we did not have that were available in cities; but, on the whole, we did all right. I look at the experiences I had growing up as moments in time which gave me the concept of right and wrong, caused me to look always for the best in people, and gave me to know that in the end most situations will turn out all right if I just do the footwork and leave the result to the Man Upstairs.

It was my good fortune to be in a village that helped raise me, and it was a rare privilege in that special time of growing up to see it from the vantage point of my Western Flyer bicycle, delivering the news, a kid pedaling away with my hair blowing in the breeze.

Afterword

A book is just words – ink applied to paper. It tells a story. Len Blackwell's recollections of life as a paperboy in Perkinston, Mississippi tells a fine story about a time and a place that is mostly gone. But he has captured the charm of the people that he came to know from those days so well that you can almost see them forever embedded in the amber of his memories.

The Perk Paperboy is an intensely personal journal about the people, places and real events that flowed through the idyllic growing-up years of its author, yet it is universal too, for those who lived in such a time as those magic years after the great war, when Americans enjoyed innocence, and when we walked confidently knowing we could do just about anything.

I'm guessing that as you turn the pages you saw people you know, and felt the warmth of remembering them, and at the end you wanted to know a little more about how it all played out for Len. Maybe he will tell us one day.

Stan Tiner is editor of the Sun Herald, the descendent of the Daily Herald that Len delivered as a boy. The Sun Herald received the 2006 Pulitzer Prize Gold Medal for Public Service for its coverage of Hurricane Katrina. Tiner is a graduate of Louisiana Tech University and was a Nieman Fellow at Harvard University. He served in the U.S. Marine Corps and was a combat correspondent during the Vietnam War.

Final Poem

Once Upon A Time

It was the last two years
Of the decade of innocence.
The clock hid its face in its hands
Time knew what was coming.
It was a time before drugs and the pill,
When our drug of choice was laughter
And our pill was an aspirin
Before the delivery of an exam.
It was time before hippies and psychedelics
When we thought we were hip
In Bass Wejuns and crew neck sweaters.
It was a time before campus riots and lock-downs
When rumor of a panty raid was our only scare.
It was a time before water hoses, dogs and billy clubs
Were unleashed on those who only wanted
To join in equal rights.
It was time when our only conflict
Was played out on a football Saturday night.
A time before over 50,000 names
Would be chiseled on a wall in Washington, DC.
It was a time before a bullet brought down
Camelot, John, Bobby and Martin
When our lives were loaded with peace.
It was time before a farm in upstate New York
Hosted a culture's last stand.
It was a time before the turbulent sixties

That would change our lives forever.
We will never forget once-upon-a-time
The fall of fifty-seven to the spring of fifty-nine.
Thank you Time for letting us
Run with the wind
Dance in our socks
Sing on our sidewalks
Respect our professors
Love our alma mater
Drink from the fountain of youth
Dream of our future
Leave our teens
Arrive as adults.
We will always owe you, Time
What an hourglass we drank from.

Margaret "Maggi" Britton Vaughn is referred to by many as "the Tennessippian." She was born in Murfreesboro, Tennessee, in 1938, moved to Gulfport, Mississippi, in the early 40's and returned to Tennessee in 1965 Maggi attended Perkinston Junior College and holds a Bachelor of Arts degree from Middle Tennessee State University.

An accomplished author, she resides in Bell Buckle, Tennessee, and travels the country as Poet Laureate of Tennessee. She read her poem "Once Upon a Time" when she was inducted into the Mississippi Gulf Coast Community College Alumni Hall of Fame in 2009, and her permission to use it here is deeply appreciated.

A Conversation with Len Blackwell

What inspired you to write the Perk Paperboy Stories?

I think I suddenly realized that the place where I grew up was very special. Several events coincided that made me feel it was almost imperative to write about everyday life in the little village of Perkinston. Since I do not believe in coincidences, I felt as though someone was tapping me on the shoulder saying, "write," sort of like what happened to the poet Caedmon. When I finally started, I found that the words came without much effort but with more feelings than I anticipated.

What events?

Mainly it was what happened one day in the fall of 2007. My brother David had come over to help me with a business matter, and we finished our work early in the day. It was one of those perfect crisp clear autumn days when there was not a cloud in the sky and the whole world seemed to be air conditioned. As we were driving back to the Mississippi Gulf Coast, David asked me to detour through the old part of the City of Wiggins. We rode by the old Stone County Courthouse and then down historic Pine Hill, which called up many pleasant memories for us. We had some extra time, so we made another detour through the village of Perkinston, where David suggested that we visit the Perkinston Cemetery. I had not been to that cemetery in many years, and when I saw the gravestones of the neighbors I knew when I was growing up, I knew at once that the few lines on their monuments were insufficient to tell their stories. Many of them had been customers on my paper route.

Then we agreed to make another detour to our family cemetery on Blackwell Farm Road in Harrison County, Mississippi. That visit did not take very long and we decided to drop in on a relative and long time friend, Mr. Preston Fayard.

Mr. Fayard was then in his mid 90s, a tall dignified thoroughly good man married to a wife who shared the sunlight of the spirit with him. Since that day he and his sweet wife have both passed from this life to a better place. The Fayards were great people.

Preston was a fine man, full of talent and native intelligence. He was an accomplished artist. I inherited one of his paintings, and it is really good. He had been a lifelong woodsman and skilled hunter and was an all around sportsman. Mrs. Fayard was a perfect lady. They defined the term "salt of the earth."

Also visiting him and his wife that day when we arrived were his daughters, some other friends and his minister. We enjoyed the fellowship and conversation over some good coffee and I soon learned that Mr. Fayard desired a private conversation with David and me. In fact, when we said that we probably should not impose on them and visit longer, his wife insisted that we stay. So when everyone else departed, we stayed.

Mrs. Fayard asked if we knew that she and Mr. Fayard had been burglarized, and we said we had not heard that unfortunate news.

"They took all of Preston's rifles and shotguns," said Mrs. Fayard. For such a renowned sportsman, I knew that was a serious event.

Mr. Fayard said that while he missed his old model 700 Remington 270 caliber rifle, he had to admit that at his age and condition it was getting to be "too much gun" for him. He also admitted to having killed a large buck the previous season, however, and when coaxed, he had color pictures to prove it. He allowed that his insurance company quickly paid for the lost property and that both the sheriff's department and the insurance agent found it remarkable that he had kept in a notebook written records of the serial numbers for each of the stolen guns.

Preston then told us that he had plans for the upcoming deer season and that he had decided after losing his guns to replace the 270 with a Remington 243 Win. We were allowed to inspect his new rifle and were impressed with its fine quality and excellent scope, an added feature that he said was desirable, given his age (mid-90s) and physical condition (frail but remarkably good, it seemed to me). I would not have bet against Mr. Fayard killing a deer that season.

"Oh, and the Sheriff caught the burglars, and they returned all my guns," Mr. Fayard added as a post script to his story. "And of course the next morning I just drove down to Gulfport to the insurance company and took them a check to reimburse them, since there was no loss," he said. After a little more conversation, we finally said our goodbyes and ended this interesting, delicious visit.

On the way home and for the next few days I kept thinking of the detours through old Wiggins, to the Perkinston Cemetery, and to see Mr. and Mrs. Fayard.

Somehow those three events compelled me to write these stories.

Are the stories true?

Yes. They are not stories I could invent, and all the characters are real. I may have embellished the facts a little and not told the whole truth in every case, but what I did tell is as true as I can remember it or as true as it was when I heard it, and I think that's pretty good for a country lawyer.

You write rather sentimentally about the village of Perkinston. How did you feel about it when you were growing up there?

I had conflicting feelings. On one hand I felt pretty safe and secure, but on the other hand I knew there was a lot more world outside our little village, and I longed to see it and be a part of it.

Why do the stories contain repetitive accounts of the same facts?

Some of them were published initially as newspaper articles so I felt that each separate article should have enough facts on any given topic to orient the reader in time, place and as to some of the important characters. I hope readers will excuse the fact that I tell everyone, for example, that I was a paperboy in Perkinston in so many of the stories, as if they didn't catch that fact in the first ten or eleven of them. I thought that if someone picked up the newspaper and read one of them for the first time, the orientation would be important, so I resorted to repetition. When the series of articles ended, I just kept the same format for this book.

Do you have plans for a Perk Paperboy sequel?

Well, I guess the paperboy could tell some more stories if I can remember more stories to tell. We could do the <u>Perk Paperboy Goes to College</u>, but I'm not sure I want to write about that yet. It wasn't so innocent.

How do you think your life after Perkinston has turned out, so far?

I'm thankful that you said "so far." I reckon my answer is "so far, so good." I think life is like playing a violin solo in Carnegie Hall while you are learning the instrument. I believe everyone does the best job possible in his or her individual case, but it is not perfect and sometimes it ain't pretty.

What lessons would you have your grandchildren take from the stories?

That the treasure is in the people you meet and know in life. That the one farthest down on the totem may pay his paper bill more reliably than the one at the top. That you can't judge anybody's insides by looking at his outsides.

Anything else?

While I'm on my bicycle, to take time and look at the scenery and stop and talk to the friends I meet along the ride. Understand that eighty percent of life is suiting up and showing up. Once you do the footwork, trust that your Higher Power is looking out for you and that His imagination is better than yours, and leave the results to him..

Why do you see small town life through such rose colored glasses?

Well, it is normal for people to look back and see the good old days as better than the times we are living in now. The ancient Romans even did it. Eric Hoffer had some interesting ideas about why we do it as we get older.

You seem overly optimistic about the future in some of your comments. Why is that?

I guess it is in my genes. Both of my parents were school teachers so they hammered into me that a good education was important. Along with that idea was the notion that we could do whatever we wanted in life. In talking to young people, I find that they still believe they can save the world, and believing it is a big part of the battle. This country needs to be investing in educating and training our young people. Everyone knows that they are the future, so if their confidence can be harnessed and cultivated we have good reason to be optimistic. I admit, however, that those are big ifs.

Did you really learn lessons on your paper route that have helped you in life?

On several occasions, yes. It was a study in character traits to see who paid on time and who didn't. Being a self-absorbed teenager, I also missed getting a lot of wisdom from the daily life in Perkinston. Looking back I realize that fact.

What would you have changed about your teenage years?

Well, since we were Baptists, I didn't learn to dance very well. In retrospect, I wouldn't have been as ambivalent about dancing, and I would have learned to dance. It is fun and should not be reserved for Annual Balls.

Any concluding words about your paperboy experience and what it meant to you?

When I pedaled my trusty Western Flyer bicycle around the village of Perkinston and met the people on my paper route at church and in school and at the lodge hall and at home, I was truly blessed to see their reflections of kindness in action. In the aggregate their good cheer and friendliness provided the atmosphere of our little village. My family and friends and customers were not perfect people. Many of them were flawed and some had grievous troubles. But on the whole they reflected a spirit which I choose to believe was a spark of the divine. I know it is easy through nostalgia to idealize those times of long ago and I know my memory is selective and imperfect, but these fellow townspeople were sweet characters who left me with sweet memories. If God made people in his own image, then the people I knew in Perkinston were that image.

I love the following passage from Emmet Fox's Power Through Constructive Thinking:

> God is the only Presence and the only Power. God is fully present here with me, now. God is the *only* real Presence—all the rest is but shadow. God is perfect Good, and God is the cause only of perfect Good. God never sends sickness, trouble, accident, temptation, nor death itself; nor does He authorize these things. We bring them upon ourselves by our own wrong thinking. God, Good, can cause only good. The same fountain cannot send forth both sweet and bitter water. I am Divine Spirit.
>
> I am the child of God. In God I live and move and have my being; so I have no fear. I am surrounded by the Peace of God and all is well. I am not afraid of people; I am not afraid of things; I am not afraid of circumstances; I am not afraid of myself; for God is with me. The Peace of God fills my soul, and I have no fear. I dwell in the Presence of God, and no fear can touch me. I am not afraid of the past; I am not afraid of the present; I am not afraid for the future; for God is with

me. The Eternal God is my dwelling place and underneath are the everlasting arms. Nothing can ever touch me but the direct action of God Himself, and God is Love.

God is Life; I understand that and I express it. God is Truth; I understand that and I express it. God is Divine Love; I understand that and I express it. I send out thoughts of love and peace and healing to the whole universe: to all trees and plants and growing things, to all beasts and birds and fishes, and to every man, woman and child on earth, without any distinction. If anyone has ever injured me or done me any kind of harm, I fully and freely forgive him now, and the thing is done with forever. I loose him and let him go. I am free and he is free. If there is any burden of resentment in me I cast it upon the Christ within, and I go free.

God is Infinite Wisdom, and that Wisdom is mine. That Wisdom leads and guides me; so I shall not make mistakes. Christ in me is a lamp unto my feet.

God is Infinite Life; and that Life is my supply; so I shall want for nothing.

God created me and He sustains me. Divine Love has foreseen everything, and provided for everything. One Mind, One Power, One Principle. One God, One Law, One Element. Closer is He than breathing, nearer than hands and feet.

I am Divine Spirit, the Child of God, and in the Presence of God I dwell forever. I thank God for Perfect Harmony.

I certainly do not claim anything like perfect adherence (or even <u>imperfect</u> adherence for that matter) to the principles in Fox's eloquent affirmation. It is way beyond my limited ability. All I am saying is that growing up in Perkinston gave me the opportunity to catch glimpses of the Divine Spirit which Fox describes through coming in contact with my neighbors' lives. They were some very dear people. Maybe sometimes God speaks through the people he places along the path of life, even to a mischievous paperboy.

Bibliography

Conroy, Pat. South of Broad. New York: Random House, Inc., 2009.

Evans, Mike. The Rock and Roll Age: The Music, The Culture, The Generation. Reader's Digest Association, Inc., 2007.

Fox, Emmet. Power Through Constructive Thinking. New York: Harper & Row, 1940.

Halbertstam, David. The Fifties. New York: Random House, Inc., 1993.

Kaplan, Fred. 1959:The Year Everything Changed. Hoboken, New Jersey: John Wiley & Sons, Inc., 2009.

Miller, James. Flowers In the Dustbin: The Rise of Rock and Roll 1947-1977. New York: Alfred A. Knopf, Inc., 1994.

Morrow, "Cousin Brucie." Doo Wop: The Music, The Times, The Era. New York: Sterling Publishing Co., Inc., 2007.

Rodriguez, Richard. Harper's Magazine, November 2009. © 2009 by Richard Rodriguez

Sullivan, Charles L. Mississippi Gulf Coast Community College: A History. Perkinston, Mississippi: Mississippi Gulf Coast Community College Press., 2002.

Ward, Geoffrey C. and Burns, Ken. Baseball: An Illustrated History. New York: Alfred A. Knopf, Inc., 1994.